When Death Enters Life

John Baum

When Death Enters Life

Floris Books

First published in Norwegian under the title
Når Døden kommer inn i Livet in 1992
Adapted from the original Norwegian by the author.
First published in English in 2003

British Library CIP Data available

ISBN 0-86315-389-5

Printed in Great Britain
by Arrowsmith, Bristol

Contents

Introduction

A human being comes to the world — a spirit descends to earth, it collects a cloud of dust around itself, clothes itself in the dust and drags it around. When its time on earth is over, the dust is laid aside and the spirit returns to the lap of eternity.[1]

Gabriel Scott (1885–1965)

A new dimension confronts us when death enters life. Instinctively we feel the need to know more about life and death. At the same time we need to make decisions in practical matters. The aim of this book is to bring experiences, observations and some practical advice, so that when we meet death we can have the possibility to be active, both spiritually and practically.

We all have our own experiences. To hear of the experiences other people have had can help us to believe in what *we* have experienced. The practical advice can be of help to see that we all can do much from where we stand in life. Often the most important thing to do is just that which we have the possibility to do, here and now.

Our point of departure is that man is a spiritual being who takes abode in the physical body on the path to birth. At death it leaves the physical body and returns to its origins. An openness for such a thought can give personal experiences an inner meaning, as well as bestowing a new dimension on life. It can also be of help when death enters life.

The book has been written for those who meet death, for those who have to face their own death, and for those who face the death of one who stands them near. The text swings from the one viewpoint to the other, perhaps it is good to experience death from different points of view? In the past thirty years the threshold of death has been enlightened by research, beginning with near-death experiences. Many years earlier Rudolf Steiner spoke on the same subject, and his research has been substantiated by many of the findings of near-death research. We have chosen to bring many sayings of wise people so that the reader, from where they stand in life, can find material which harmonizes with his own experiences. The aim is that everyone will feel free to ponder and wonder about death, and therefore about life.

In 1992 the book *Når Døden kommer inn i Livet* was published in Norway, which I wrote with Dagny Bartz-Johannessen. That book arose though a working together of doctors, priests, nurses, social workers and other experienced people who themselves had met death and worked with death in their daily lives.The aim was to formulate something to give to people who met death, so that they could work on themselves and be active. Dagny Bartz-Johannessen, with her rich life experience, has also advised and helped with the forming of this book. She has a gift of bringing the contents "down to earth" and is hereby thanked for all help.

Karin Medböe, priest in the Christian Community in Botton Village in England, took the initiative that the book should be reworked in the English language. She has followed the progress of the book, advising and helping, especially to find many of the sayings. Peter Button, through his many years of experience as a priest in the Christian Community, has helped form the contents, contributing, correcting and advising. Karin Medböe and Peter Button's help has been decisive in enabling this book to be available in English. They are hereby thanked for their invaluable help and encouragement.

Over many years Friedwart Bock has noted nature's response to human death. His observations corresponded with mine. Thanks also for his help through correspondence and with translating.

Many people have contributed, translating texts, finding contents and through conversations. Hearty thanks to all. We are always grateful to hear of experiences, and receive contents that can be of help to others when meeting death.

I have described religious rituals from where I stand in life, as priest in the Christian Community. Members of other denominations will needs include the rituals of their church or religion in the framework of the book.

To my wife, Gerd Eva, a special word of thanks for her support and encouragement.

John Baum
May 2003

1. Approaching Death

At the age of seventy-five ... one must, of course,
think sometimes of death. But this thought never
gives me the least uneasiness, for I am fully
convinced that our spirit is a being of a nature
quite indestructible, and that its activity continues
from eternity to eternity. It is like the sun, which
seems to set only to our earthly eyes, but which, in
reality, never sets, but shines on unceasingly.[1]

Johann Wolfgang von Goethe (1749–1832)

Death is a part of life. All who have been present at the birth
or the death of a human being will have divined something of
the greatness of such an event. It is as if a door is opened for
a moment and we can glance into another world. In such
moments we speak quietly, are filled with reverence, and
experience more than meets the eye.

At the same time meeting with death can come as a shock.
Death can come as lightning from a clear sky, an accident, a
heart that stops beating. Or we hear that the time with our
loved one will be short when a serious illness is diagnosed. It
is not easy to believe. We live in hope. We try all we can. But
there comes the time when we stand face to face with death.

What can we do? How can we prepare ourselves and our
loved ones for what we know will come? How can we find the
courage to meet that which comes towards us? If death is
approaching due to illness, how can we shape the last weeks
or months in a positive manner?

It is perhaps not necessary to talk so much about what is
approaching, but to have knowledge, and try to help each
other accept the situation. This can give a new sense of shar-

ing which can be of help later, for this experience of community transcends time and space.

Many have experienced that they are in a special life situation, both before and afterwards, when they have to meet death. One often has much to do in everyday life. At the same time one lives in a kind of threshold landscape. One's senses are sharper for what is real and true; we see what is of importance; we can sense that moments are precious.

Perhaps we can try, just for a short time in the evening, to put aside the tiredness we feel, the worry we bear, and the pain, and turn to something beautiful, to something that has an intrinsic value. Perhaps we can contemplate a crystal, or look at a piece of art. In the crystal, in the work of art, we can divine the inherent *idea* which comes to expression in the particular earthly manifestation.

We can light a candle. Read something together — a poem, a favourite book, or a passage from the Bible, if that feels comfortable. Music builds a bridge from the one world to the next. It may be of help to listen to music, to play music, or to sing.

We can try to create moments of quality in a difficult period. The experience of community that can arise can be of help to bear us through, and help us to meet what must be met. Such moments help build a bridge from soul to soul. Dag Hammarskjöld (1905–61) wrote:

> The dust settles heavily, the air becomes stale, the
> light dim in the room which we are not prepared to
> leave at any moment.
>   Your body must become familiar with its death —
> in all its possible forms and degrees — as a self-evident, imminent, and emotionally neutral step on the
> way towards the goal you have found worthy of your
> life.[2]

Upside-down, inside-out[3]

by Peter Button

What is it like to live in an upside-down world? Paul Gallico describes just such an experience in his novel about the wreck of the ship, *Poseidon*. Because of a seaquake, this great liner is suddenly completely overturned. The survivors below deck, after their first shock, slowly realize that they must radically reorientate themselves. The tables and chairs are suspended upside-down, clamped to the floor which is now the ceiling. The electric lights now shine up from under their feet. The staircases are reversed and can no longer be climbed. Some of the passengers are able to realize what has happened and gradually find their way about in the new situation. Others are completely disorientated and are incapable of any action at all.

Fortunately such experiences rarely come the way of human beings, but a comparable and perhaps even stronger experience will come to every human being at the moment of death. During life on earth, our human spirit is enclosed within our physical body. Most people when seriously asked where they think their spirit is, will reply "Somewhere inside me."

At death, the physical body has fulfilled its task and is set free by the soul and spirit. The spirit is then no longer within the body but outside it. Sometimes a person, seeing for the first time the body of a friend or relative who has died, will say, "That is not Mike, Mike isn't there any more." This is a realization that the spirit of their friend is no longer enclosed by their body. For our normal earthly experience it is like a turning inside-out. It is a process, which can begin before death. When someone is near death, he sometimes asks the friends around the bedside why they are going away, and the friends are surprised because they have been there all along. The explanation is that the one who is dying has already begun to leave his body, and from his point of view, his friends are consequently more distant.

When we are within our physical body what we experience appears as one thing after another during the course of time. Immediately after death we find ourselves living in a host of memories of our life, not as a sequence in time, but as though all of them were there at once. Some of those who have narrowly escaped death by drowning describe how they *saw* their whole life flash before them. They *see* it as though it is there in space, and not in time as it was when the events first took place. This memory picture is seen quite objectively and without the illusions that we often cherish about ourselves in life. We can have illusions about ourselves as long as we rely only on our own point of view. Robert Burns in his ode "To a Louse" which is crawling on the hat of a proud, vain woman in church while she is completely unaware of it, says:

O wad some power the giftie gie us
Te see oursels as others see us!

In fact we do have the gift of seeing ourselves as others see us, at least partially, if we want to use it, nor is it necessary to wait until after death. It depends first on seeing rightly the things around us. If we look at a tree, we see one aspect of it. If we look at it from another angle, we see another aspect. There are many aspects to one tree. If we look at the same tree in the spring, it will look quite different from what it did in the autumn. A tree has so many different aspects in space and also in time. If we extend this way of looking and thinking to other things, we become aware that there is more than appears at first glance in all that is around us. When we also think about other people in this way, we begin to understand others much better. We become aware of the relationship between other people and ourselves. What other people do and feel and think has an effect on us. What we do and feel and think, similarly, has an effect on others. Our awareness of others is deepened and this in turn helps us to see ourselves as others see us. It gives us a better orientation in life. We are able to become more objective about ourselves and more prepared for the changes that take place at death.

What has been described as the memory picture, which occurs after death, lasts for about three days. It is followed by a further expansion into the soul world when our life on earth is more deeply evaluated. We will also experience the effect of our earthly actions on other human beings — from the other person's point of view.

One who is well prepared for death is one who is also well prepared for life.

Positive preparation for the future

Oh Lord, grant me
The serenity to accept the things I cannot change,
the courage to change the things I can
and the wisdom to know the difference.[4]

Christoph Friedrich Oetinger (1702–82)

When we are going on a long journey, there is always much to prepare. One not only has to prepare for the journey; one wants to also arrange as much as possible for those who stay at home. Many will experience just that when they prepare for their last journey, the greatest of them all.

It is possible to prepare, in the midst of life, quietly and in a positive way, for the time when we will be leaving life. To give something up, to give something away that we are attached to, are exercises in life to prepare for death.

It is not easy for everyone to speak about what is close to their heart, especially if they are ill and weak. It is therefore important for those close to one who is near death to listen carefully. Often in small remarks we can hear what the person wishes. Perhaps he wishes to meet a person, to make up before the chance has gone.

Perhaps the one dying has thoughts about a post mortem, or donation of organs? Perhaps the one dying has thought through the question of burial or cremation? There are many who have special wishes for music and songs for the burial, or for a celebration after the burial. As one younger woman said, shortly before she died, "After the burial I want you all to have a good time."

There may be special wishes about their possessions, Perhaps the one dying wishes to give a present to a friend, the children or grandchildren. It is always good for the bereaved if the deceased has already in life decided about his earthly possessions. To make a Will is of help to give away earthly possessions which one has accumulated through life. The word *Will* is a wonderful. To make up one's mind and writes one's *Will*. The impulses, which we *will* will live on, thanks to our Will. An old Will was introduced by the words:

> Nothing is more certain than death
> And nothing more uncertain than the hour of death.

It is good to write down your wishes in the event of your death. It is of great help for those who are left behind.

Post Mortem. Are there special wishes?
Donation of organs. Special wishes?
Funeral. Burial or cremation?
Ritual, of which denomination?
Music, special wishes?
Memorial meeting, special wishes?
Place of grave (give details).
Is a Will written? If so, where is it kept?
Other wishes

Remember to sign and date the document.

Peter Button wrote:

> There are two events which give people a greater awareness of a spiritual world than usual. One is the birth of a child, or being in the presence of a newly born child; the other is the death of a human being, or shortly before death takes place and for a few days afterwards. These are moments of crossing over from one world to the other, and so powerful are they that

those around them are affected by them and become a little more open to the world from which the child comes, the world into which the dying person enters.

Birth is not a sudden event; preparations are made over the proceeding months, and spiritual preparations possibly over a considerably longer period. Death, too, is generally not a sudden event, and for everyone it is a certainty. Preparation, not only from the outer physical, social and economic side, but also from a spiritual aspect, is possible and desirable.

When someone is dying there is often a tendency for the friends, relatives and sometimes doctors to refrain from mentioning the fact, or even to deny that death is imminent. One man, to whom the doctor had admitted he was suffering from terminal cancer, asked how long he might expect to live. The doctor was very reluctant to answer this question and commit himself, but the man said to him, "Look, I have answered hundreds of your questions, you answer this one."

Under this pressure the doctor admitted that the patient had a life expectancy of about four months.

The man thanked him, saying, "Now I know where I stand. I can put my things in order and be prepared for death."

This is really the attitude of a mature person; to want to make conscious preparation for death.[5]

To live with the Sacraments in a religious context can be part of the positive preparation for meeting death. Of significance is the Sacramental Consultation, as practised in the Christian Community — where the individual can look back over life, and strive for strength to meet that which comes towards him. Also Holy Communion can be a blessing. In some churches, in the Christian Community and in the Catholic Church, there is a special sacrament for those who close to death, the Last Anointing.

Even though there are many questions that arise at a

deathbed, it is important that an atmosphere of peace, harmony and love surrounds the one dying. Not all questions can be answered. There is a time and a place for all. A certain sensitivity is needed. Many years ago an old farmer was dying. He had been unconscious for some days, and the family gathered around him. While waiting they started to talk about what would happen to the farm after he died. It did not take long before he was conscious and made clear to all who was still in charge!

A young nurse was told to go to an unconscious patient with a Christmas card. She stood there with the card, and felt a little silly while she read the greetings. At that moment she saw a tear fall down the cheek of the unconscious person.

A person, who stands at the gate of death has many similarities to a newborn child. Both are part of the world they come from, and the world they are going to. The child sleeps and gradually wakes up more and more. The dying one often appears to dose and sleep. They may have experiences that reach over our earthly ones. Shortly before he died a wise old man tried to fathom what he was experienced: "I see mythological pictures." Did he begin to sense the loosening from his body and the mythological pictures he experienced were released by this loosening. The Norwegian writer Johan Falkberget (1879–1967), when near death, experienced that his dead ones came near. His daughter, Aasta Falkberget, has related:

> One morning when we came down to him he told us quite naturally, and with a clearer voice than he had had for a long time: "I have spoken to your mother today."
>
> I was surprised but asked, so as not to disappoint him: "What did she look like?"
>
> Without hesitating he answered: "I did not see her, but she was happy and satisfied." Father smiled happily. It was a long time since I had seen him smile.

The nearer he came to the boundaries of life the more
clairvoyant he became ...
When he waved out into the air and smiled, he
said to us: "Can you not see them?"
If we gave no sign that we *saw* the same as he saw
he was quite frustrated.
"They are all standing there," he would say.
Once, when he waved to the unknown, I asked him
with my mouth to his ear: "Whom do you see now?"
He turned his head to me and whispered "Father."
And both of us waved to my grandfather; my father
with eyes that *saw,* and I with eyes which could not
see more than the wall with a picture hanging on it.[6]

On the surface of a swift-flowing stream the reflections of things near or far are always indistinct; even
if the water is clear and has no foam. Reflections in
the constant stream of ripples, the restless kalei-
descope of water, are still uncertain, vague, incompre-
hensible.

Only when the water has flowed down river after
river and reaches a broad, calm estuary or comes to
rest in some backwater or a small, still lake — only
then can we see in its mirror-like smoothness every
leaf of a tree on the bank, every wisp of a cloud and
the deep blue expanse of the sky.

It is the same with our lives. If so far we have been
unable to see clearly or to reflect the eternal linea-
ments of truth, is it not because we too are still moving towards some end — because we are still alive?[7]
Aleksander Solzhenitsyn (born 1918)

2. The Moment of Death

*On earth, death has a terrifying aspect only
because we look upon it as a kind of dissolution,
as an end. But when we look back upon the
moment of death from the other side, from the
spiritual side, then death continually appears to
us as a victory of the spirit, as the Spirit that is
extricating itself from the physical. It then
appears as the greatest, most beautiful and
significant event. Moreover, this experience kindles
that which constitutes our ego-consciousness after
death.*[1]

Rudolf Steiner (1861–1925)

Peter Button wrote:

Some people are helped by the presence of other human
beings in these last moments on earth. Others need to
be alone. A degree of sensitivity is necessary here in
order to know what is appropriate. Those who stay can
share a little in what is experienced inwardly by the
dying person, and may also attend to the bodily necess-
ities. At home one can usually create the right atmosphere. In a large hospital ward this may not be so easy,
and there friends and relatives must be able to accept
that life around them and outer activity are — rightly
— going on. One visitor to a hospital ward became very
upset because she heard nurses in another part of the
ward laughing together. She said, "My mother is dying,
and those nurses can only laugh." But it would be
almost impossible for nurses to do their work if they
had to retain a constantly solemn face when they are

working with the dying. In this sense the dying are not so sensitive; they appreciate having cheerful faces around them and they are happy to know that others are experiencing the joys of existence and that the world does and will go on after they leave it.

If one is granted the grace to be present at the actual moment of death it is appropriate to say quietly the words of the Lord's Prayer. Then come the many practical activities, which must take, place, including calling the doctor, the priest or minister, and the funeral director.

The spirit has struggled for the whole of its life on earth to work in this physical body and the end of life is the sign that what had to be done in and with this physical body is completed and the spirit can finally withdraw from it. The spirit leaves its mark especially on the countenance, and when one looks at one who has died one can so often be amazed at the great peace and tranquillity that has settled on the peaceful countenance; or at other times one can see the great nobility of feature in one who had been thought of as a fairly simple person. What has not shown itself in life is often revealed in death.

Outwardly the moment of death may seem grotesque because of the pain or inability to control all the bodily movements, but what the soul is experiencing is something much greater. Sometimes one has inklings of it when, after what seemed particularly hard struggles, the dying person returns to consciousness and says the he has seen the "golden gates." That is a pictorial expression for the spiritual threshold. Those near to death often speak pictorially (as Elisabeth Kübler-Ross testifies), and one needs to be aware that "going home," for instance, is not necessarily a reference to going back to the home from the hospital, but to the journey to the spiritual home to which the dying look forward.[2]

The Swedish poet Karin Boye (1900–1941) in her poem: "Yes, of course it hurts," gives a telling image of death. She describes the buds breaking open and the freeing of the flower. Death can be a painful process — often accompanied by a death struggle. It looks painful and difficult to those around the one dying. For the one who is dying it may be felt differently. As death approaches that what gives life to the physical body, the life body or ether body begins to loosen from the physical body. This is what is seen as the death struggle. The dying person experiences above all the freeing of the soul and spirit.

Yes, of course it hurts

Yes, of course it hurts when buds are breaking.
Why else would the springtime falter?
Why would all our ardent longing
bind itself in frozen, bitter pallor?
After all, the bud was covered all the winter.
What new thing is it that bursts and wears?
Yes, of course it hurts when buds are breaking,
hurts for that which grows
                and that which bars.

Yes, it is hard when drops are falling.
Trembling with fear, and heavy hanging,
cleaving to the twig, and swelling, sliding –
weight draws them down, though they go on clinging.
Hard to be uncertain, afraid and divided,
hard to feel the depths attract and call,
yet sit fast and merely tremble —
hard to want to stay
                and want to fall.

Then, when things are worst and nothing helps
the tree's buds break as in rejoicing,
then, when no fear holds back any longer,
down in glitter go the twig's drops plunging,

forget that they were frightened by the new,
forget their fears before the flight unfurled –
feel for a second their greatest safety,
rest in that trust
    that creates the world.

                    Karin Boye[3]

I am standing on the seashore. A ship at my side
spreads her white sails to the morning breeze and
starts for the blue ocean. She is an object of
beauty and strength, and I stand and watch her
until at length she is a speck of white cloud just where
the sea and sky come to mingle with each other.
    Then someone at my side says, "There! She's
gone!" Gone where? Gone from my sight, that is all.
She is just as large in mast and hull and spar as
she was when she left my side, and she is just as
able to bear her load of living weight to her destined
harbor.
    Her diminished size is in me, not in her. And just
at the moment when someone at my side says, There!
She's gone! there are other eyes watching her coming,
and other voices ready to take up the glad shout,
"There she comes!"

                Henry Jackson van Dyke (1852–1933)

Percy Bysshe Shelley

The circumstances around Shelley's death were strange.
Before he died Shelley saw a spirit appear out of the waves,
smiling to him in the moonlight. He was visited by a spirit
which had his own appearance who asked, "How much longer
are you going to be satisfied by this?"
    On July 8, 1822, on what was to be the last day of his life,
Shelley sailed out with Captain Williams in the boat *Ariel*. It

was good weather, a slight breeze blew. Through binoculars his friend, Trelawny, saw *Ariel* leave the shore. The sea, he related, looked calm and and was covered by an oil-like foam. The wind blew over the surface without breaking it up. The storm lasted twenty minutes. Some days later the bodies were washed ashore. Hunt and Lord Byron helped Trelawny to burn the bodies. Oil was thrown over them and a special burial ritual were read: "I give back to Nature through the cleansing fire the elements this man was made of: earth, air and water. All is transformed, but not destroyed. He is now part of that which he worshipped.[5]

William Blake

William Blake's last hour struck on that 12th August of 1827: With a strong, feeling voice he sang again to welcome death; now and then he uttered his last words: "My beloved, I am going to that country which I have all my life wished to see. I am happy, hoping for salvation through Jesus Christ; but we shall not be parted. I shall always be about you to take care of you ..."

Then, at about six in the evening, his countenance became fair, his eyes brightened, and he burst out singing again of the things he saw in heaven. Then a brief silence ensued and quietly he passed from life on earth into eternal Life.[6]

A farmer's death

Elisabeth Kübler-Ross (born 1926) relates, from her childhood, of a farmer's death:

He was a farmer, probably in his fifties ... His death came after he fell from an apple tree and broke his neck, but it did not kill him immediately. At the hospital doctors told him they were helpless, and so he insisted on being sent home to die. There was plenty of time for his family, relatives and friends to say goodbye. On the day we went, he was surrounded by his family and children. His room overflowed with wildflowers, and his bed was positioned so that he could look out the window on his fields and fruit trees, literally the fruits of his labor that would survive the drift of time. The dignity and love and peace I saw made a lasting impression.

The next day he died, and we returned that afternoon to view his body. I was a very reluctant participant, not eager at all for the experience of the lifeless body ... But the viewing turned out to be a fascinating moment. Gazing at his body, I realized that he was no longer there. Whatever force or energy gave him life, whatever it was that we mourned, had vanished.[7]

Sophie Scholl

Sophie Scholl was executed in Munich on February 22, 1943 for resistance activity at the University in Munich. Together with her friends in the resistance group, the White Rose, she had been arrested, tried and now awaited execution. When Sophie woke after her last night, she told her cellmate the dream she had dreamt:

One morning I carried a Child in a long white dress to its christening. To get to church we had to go up the steep side of a mountain. But the Child lay safely in my arms. Suddenly a deep crevasse opened in front of me. I just managed to cast the Child over to the other side — before I fell down into the depth."

She elucidated the simple dream for her cellmate in the following manner: "The Child is the idea we

have striven for. We have prepared the path for it, and
it will be able to live. But, so that it can win, we
must die.[8]

Kim Malte-Bruun

Kim Malthe-Bruun was sentenced to death for resistance
activity in Denmark and executed on April 6, 1945. Two days
before his execution the young man wrote to his mother:

Dear Mother:
Today, together with Jörgen, Nils, and Ludwig, I was
arraigned before a military tribunal. We were condemned to death. I know that you are a courageous
woman, and that you will bear this, but, hear me, it is
not enough to bear it, you must also understand it. I
am an insignificant thing, and my person will soon be
forgotten, but the thought, the life, the inspiration that
filled me will live on. You will meet them everywhere
— in the trees at springtime, in people who cross your
path, in a loving little smile. You will encounter that
something which perhaps had value in me, you will
cherish it, and you will not forget me. And so I shall
have a chance to grow, to become large and mature. I
shall be living with all of you whose hearts I once
filled. And you will all live on, knowing that I have
preceded you, and not, as perhaps you thought at first,
dropped out behind you. You know what my dearest
wish has always been, and what I hoped to become.
Follow me, my dear mother, on my path, and do not
stop before the end, but linger with some of the matters belonging to the last space of time allotted to me,
and you will find something that may be of value both
to my sweetheart and to you, my mother.
    I travelled a road that I have never regretted. I have
never evaded the dictate of my heart, and now things

seem to fall into place. I am not old, I should not be dying, yet it seems so natural to me, so simple. It is only the abrupt manner of it that frightens us at first. The time is short, I cannot properly explain it, but my soul is perfectly at rest ...

The same day he wrote to his girl friend:

My own Little Sweetheart:
Today I was put on trial and condemned to death. What terrible news for a girl only twenty years old. I obtained permission to write this farewell letter. And what shall I write now? What notes are to go into this, my swan song? The time is short, and there are so many thoughts. What is the final and most precious gift that I can make to you? What do I possess that I can give you in farewell, in order that you may live on, grow, and become an adult, in sorrow and yet with a happy smile?

We sailed upon the wild sea, we met each other in the trustful way of playing children, and we loved each other. We still love each other and we shall continue to do so. But one day a storm tore us asunder; I struck a reef and went down, but you were washed up on another shore, and you will live on in a new world. You are not to forget me, I do not ask that; why should you forget something that is so beautiful? But you must not cling to it. You must live on as gay as ever and doubly happy, for life has given you on your path the most beautiful of all beautiful things. Tear yourself free; let this joy be all for you, let it radiate as the strongest and clearest force in the world, but let it be only one of your golden remembrances; don't let it blind you and so prevent you from seeing all the glorious things that lie still before you ...

You will live on and meet with other marvellous adventures ...

Lift up your head, my heart's most precious core,
lift up your head and look about you. The sea is still
blue — the sea that I have loved so much, the sea that
has enveloped both of us. Live on now for the two of
us. I am gone and far away, and what remains is not a
memory that should turn you into a woman like N.N.,
but a memory that should make you into a woman
who is alive and warm-hearted, mature and happy. You
must not bury yourself in sorrow, for you would be
arrested, ... and you would lose what I have loved
most in you, your womanliness. Remember, and I
swear to you that it is true, that every sorrow turns
into happiness — but very few people will in retrospect
admit this to themselves. They wrap themselves in
their sorrow, and habit leads them to believe that it
continues to be sorrow, and they go on wrapping themselves up in it. The truth is that after sorrow comes a
maturation, and after maturation comes fruit.[9]

Monique's death

Margje Koster interviewed seven people with Aids. Monique
told about her life and her having to meet death at 28. She
told about her hard childhood and of her time together with
a drug addict, and how after his death she learnt that he had
AIDS and that she was infected. With her new friend, Rob, she
prepares for her death:

I am busy arranging my funeral on paper and telling
people my wishes, for example, by choosing music.
That's very difficult because there is so much beatiful
music. The other day Rob said that if they played
everything that I had chosen, they would have to sit
in the funeral parlour for three days. It made me
laugh, I can just see it.
I would like a purple coffin, with a beautiful lining.

I would also like to be laid out at home with many flowers and my toy rabbit in the coffin, because it was always a source of comfort to me.

Rob can make a speech and I hope that he says that he misses me because that will mean that he loved me. Also I was always open to people, because I think that's a very important quality, particularly when you're ill. Many people around me who also have AIDS are only concerned with themselves, so they have little understanding for other people. I would like to urge them all to love each other and listen to each other because that's what life is all about.

I don't understand my fate. I keep looking to understand why this happened, but I can't find the answer. I'll only find the answer when I'm dead. I'll knock and they'll open up for me and then I can ask: "Why? What is it that makes me deserve this?" and then I will finally know ...

[Monique became very ill, and could see no reasons to live, apart from her friend Rob's birthday.]

On Rob's birthday she told the doctor she didn't want to go on. She was very ill and had a very high fever. It was arranged with the doctor that on Wednesday (this was on Monday) she would get help if she were still there.

In order to discuss her worries about the possibility of euthanasia, a priest was called to put her mind at rest, and then she asked to be christened. This is what happened. Monique was christened in Rob's arms and then received the last rites. Monique was radiant with joy. All those who were present were moved. Then she became calm and was able to surrender completely. During the following night her mind was clear and she was calm. She communicated intensely with her mother and with Rob. In the morning at a quarter past nine, it became clear that the moment of departure was at hand.

Rob was with her and he told us: "Suddenly the birds in the garden began to sing. I looked at Monique and said: 'Can you hear them?' Monique nodded: 'They are calling you,' I said. 'I think that it's time to go, my little angel. We've had a good time together but now we have to say goodbye. Go on, don't worry about me, everything will be alright.' She looked at me once more and then breathed her last breath. Then at the same moment the candle next to Monique, which had been lit by the priest when she was christened, went out. This happened on May 12 at twenty-three minutes past nine.

"I looked into her eyes, and as long as I live, I will remember what I saw there at the moment of death. I saw that Monique could see something which she had never seen before. She saw something entirely new, and this made her eyes shine in an indescribable way. I have never believed that there was anything after death, but through her I caught a glimpse of the world on the other side and I am one hundred per cent sure that she's happy there."

According to her wishes, Monique was laid out at home in her purple coffin. We watched over her for three days and nights. The atmosphere around her was light and peaceful. It was a privilege to all of us to experience this. Of course there was also a great deal of sadness but the main feeling was one of peace and gratitude.[10]

Postcard

Floris Books
15 Harrison Gardens
Edinburgh
EH11 1SH
United Kingdom

If you are interested in other publications from Floris Books, please return this card with your name and address.

Name _____ Surname _____

Address _____

_____

_____ Postcode _____

I am interested in the following subjects:

☐C Celtic
☐R Religion
☐S Science
☐H Health & parenting
☐J Children's books
☐A Crafts & activities

E-mail: _____

☐ Please send me your catalogue ONCE
☐ Please send me your catalogue REGULARLY
☐ Please E-mail me about new books in future

If you are in North America, our distributor, Anthroposophic Press, will send their catalogue to you.

I found this card in: _____

Book title

PC-0107

Floris Books

3. The Three Days Following Death

Even as natural life conceals death, so death reveals true life. Do we not experience it again and again through those who are dying that death's nearness allows the true nature of man, hidden behind so many masks and sheaths, to flash forth momentarily? Did we ever imagine that such majesty can slumber in a wretched, sinful human being? And when the soulless body lies on the bier and we are moved deeply enough, do we not gain knowledge through compassion? Is it not given to us then to seek and find the spirit-form that struggles free of the body? Certainly, times will come when pain will cause people to become aware of the soul-spiritual part of the one of whose presence death had robbed them.[1]

Emil Bock (1895–1959)

When a close relative or friend dies, the whole of our consciousness is centred on our loved one. To be able to cope with the situation in a good way, we need to have our feet well planted on the ground, and need to take care to get enough sleep and have regular meals.

Although the soul departs with the last breath, it is still near the bodily house in which it has dwelt over the years and it seems to remain near over the next three or four days. Almost unconsciously we tread more lightly and speak more softly in the room where there is one who has died, for something of

the calm surrounding that soul can be felt. All the
experiences that have taken place in and with that
body are somehow still there, all around it. Some of
those who have had the shock of a near-death experience have spoken of how they saw the whole of
their lives before them like one great panorama. It is
not difficult to imagine that this panorama, this
great memory picture, is experienced strongly by the
one who has really died in the days immediately following death. Those who visit during those days
share in those memories, remember themselves the
times when they were with that person, and remember also things that he or she had told them about
their life.[2]

Seeing the deceased

Adults must decide for themselves whether they wish to see
the body or not. For children it is different, adults have to
decide for them. Whether a child should see the body, depends
very much on their age and individuality, the conditions
around the death and, not least, the adult's attitude towards
death. It may, however, be more difficult for the child to be
kept away, than to be allowed to take a proper farewell to a
beloved grandparent. An adult, who experiences the greatness of death may well manage to give the child a light-filled
experience, despite the sorrow the child feels. The image of
the butterfly leaving the cocoon may be a good preparation
for a small child.

A five year old boy spent some time at the open coffin of
his grandfather while it stood in the grandparents' home. The
following year his other grandfather died. Now six years old,
the boy went to the funeral but was not to be comforted, as
he had not said "farewell" to this grandfather.

After a fatal bus accident a father was advised not to see
his daughter who was badly injured. Nevertheless he wished

to see her. He stood quietly by his daughter for a long time. Then he said: "She is so beautiful!"

The doctor responsible reflected later: "I have never heard a negative comment in such a situation. But I have been thanked for help to take leave. Therefore my advice to all those who miss a loved one is: Take time to sit with the one who has died."[3]

The watch

A Death

"His face shone" she said,
"Three days I had him in my house,
Three days before they took him from his bed,
And never have I felt so close."

"Always alive he was
A little drawn away from me.
Looks are opaque when living and his face
Seemed hiding something, carefully."

"But those three days before
They took his body out, I used to go
And talk to him. That shining from him bore
No secrets. Living he never looked or answered so."

Sceptic, I listened, then
Noted what peace she seemed to have,
How tenderly she put flowers on his grave
But not as if he might return again
Or shine or seem quite close:
Rather to please us were the flowers she gave.

Elizabeth Jennings

It was the custom in rural areas many years ago that after a death, family, friends and neighbours gathered around the coffin which was kept at home for the first few days. One held watch over the deceased. Perhaps one sensed that much still happened during the days after death? Perhaps one felt that it was possible to accompany the deceased on his way when those nearest him were around him for the first days after death. After some days the lid was placed on the coffin and the deceased, after a short ceremony was taken to where the burial was to be held.

It is possible to watch over our loved one. It can be a gift, which later in life one may think back to in gratitude.

Ask for a place in a hospital; many also have their own chapel. Some congregations may make a room available for the watch if the deceased has been part of a congregation. Or it may be good to arrange to have the coffin brought home and make a place there.

The room where the coffin is placed should be well ventilated and not too warm. To freshen the air it is possible to have a small saucer or an open bottle with eucalyptus or rosemary oil.

Flowers can be laid directly around the coffin, some around the deceased. They will wither after they have given of their beauty. In this way the withering flowers will be a living picture of the process the deceased goes through when the life forces withdraw.

It is possible to see, especially in the facial features, that there is a marked change in the course of the three days after death. There comes a point when the body seems, in some way, deserted. The time has come to cover the face with a cloth and to put the lid onto the coffin. It is very individual when this moment is reached, depending to some extent on the cause of death. It is always possible to put the cloth on the face if the situation warrants it, for example if the death is caused by an accident.

In an atmosphere of calm and beauty our thoughts can follow the deceased a little on the way. We can think back on our common experiences, and experience gratitude for the good times we have had together. Perhaps we feel the need to read from the Bible.

What happens in the three days?

> The things that flashed back came in the order of my
> life, and they were so vivid. The scenes were just like
> you walked outside and saw them, completely three-
> dimensional, and in color. And they moved. For
> instance, when I saw myself breaking the toy, I could
> see all the movements. It wasn't like I was watching it
> all from my perspective at the time. It was like the lit-
> tle girl I saw was somebody else, in a movie, one little
> girl among all the other children out there playing on
> the playground. Yet, it was me. I saw myself doing
> these things, as a child, and they were the exact same
> things I had done, because I remember them.[4]

When we observe a crystal and admire its beautiful form, we
know that it will keep its form for an eternity. The physical
formative forces which have formed the crystal form the lifeless material.

If we observe a flower, or another living being, we know
that the form is there for a limited time. When the flower
withers, or an animal dies, the living form will slowly be lost.
We can call that which gives life, the "life body" or "etheric
body" as it is also termed.

Rudolf Steiner spoke often about death and life after
death. Speaking over fifty years before near-death experiences began to be described by researchers, Steiner
described many of the same phenomena. The terminology
Steiner uses is developed in his book, *Theosophy*. To
describe the supersensory, Steiner carefully delineates and
defines the terms he uses. He tried to approach the theme of
death in varied ways:

> When a person dies ... the etheric body then leaves
> him, as well as the astral body and Ego. These three
> bodies rise away and for a time remain united. At the
> moment of death the connection between the astral

body and etheric body, on the one hand, and the physical body, on the other hand, is broken ...

The actual instant of death brings a remarkable
experience: for a brief space of time the person
remembers all that has happened to him in the life
just ended. His entire life appears before his soul in a
moment, like a great tableau. Something like this can
happen during life, in rare moments of great shock or
anger — for instance a man who is drowning, or
falling from a great height, when death seems imminent, may see his whole life before him in this way ...

The etheric body is the bearer of memory; the more
strongly developed it is, the stronger a person's faculty
of memory will be. While the etheric body is firmly
rooted in the physical body, as normally it is, its
vibrations cannot act on the brain sufficiently to
become conscious, because the physical body with its
coarser rhythms conceals them. But in moments of
deadly danger the etheric body is loosened, and with
its memories it detaches itself from the brain and a
man's whole life flashes before his soul. At such
moments everything that has been inscribed on the
etheric body reappears; hence also the recollection of
the whole past life immediately after death. This lasts
for some time, until the etheric body separates from
the astral body and the Ego."[5]

Rudolf Steiner has described the length of time, which the
life body (etheric body) needs to loosen itself from the physical body as about three days, or the time someone might be
able to stay awake without the regeneration which sleep
brings. Then the life body is set aside, discarded, as a second
corpse, the first being the physical body.

4. The Burial

Death is not an end, but a beginning. It is but an incident in the "life of the ages," which is God's gift to us now. It is the escape of the spirit from its old limitations and its freeing for a larger and more glorious career. We stand around the grave, and as we take our last, lingering look, too often our thoughts are there; and we return to the desolate home feeling that all that made life lovely has been left behind on the bleak hillside ... Yet the spirit now is free, and the unseen angel at our side points upwards from the grave and whispers, "He is not here, but is risen." The dear one returns with us to our home, ready and able, as never before, to comfort, encourage, and beckon us onwards.[1]

William Littleboy

After the three days, the time has come for the body to be given back to the earth. This is expressed in the Old Testament (Gen.3:19):

> Till you return to the ground,
> for out of it you were taken;
> you are dust,
> and to dust you shall return.

This is the motive of the Protestant burial service, where earth is cast onto the coffin and in a ritual form the words are spoken.

Also in the Old Testament (Eccles.12:7) a further motive is spoken of:

> And the dust returns to the earth as it was, and the
> spirit return to God who gave it.

This is the motive in the burial service in the Christian Community. At the place where the body is given over to the elements, we turn in thought and prayer to the deceased, to where the dead one's soul and spirit are.

If the deceased has wished for burial or cremation, all is clear. If no wish has been uttered, those left behind must decide. Is there a difference between burial and cremation for the deceased? Does it matter for the deceased what happens to the discarded body?

We know that the body will disintegrate and return to the earth. With burial the process will take a longer time. The coffin will be placed in the earth and the body will slowly become part of the earth in a very slow combustion process. With cremation the body is given over to fire and after some hours the bodily form is no more — ash remains. The ash is placed in an urn which is placed in the ground. After a time the urn, which is usually made today of metal that corrodes relatively rapidly, falls away and the ash becomes part of the earth.

We can ponder over the difference between burial and cremation. Perhaps when a person has died suddenly, or was very connected to his body and the material world, it is better that the bodily form is not obliterated rapidly? Perhaps it is different for a very old person, or for someone whose consciousness in life had already loosened the connections to the body?

In the funeral service the priest or minister, or someone who knew the person well, can give a portrait of the deceased. Every person is unique, every life special. At death it may be possible to see threads of destiny which are hidden in life.

Music can help so that the ceremony is objective and directed to the deceased. The music can help underline the greatness of the closing of a person's life on earth. But music needs to be chosen carefully so that it does not call forth sentimentality. It then does not help the deceased or those present.

It can sometimes be a question whether the funeral should be held "quietly." Grief can be hard for those left behind, and it may seem to be a good choice to let the burial take place quietly. On the other hand, every person has left their mark, often far beyond the circle of relatives. It can be hard for those who cannot follow their friend on the last journey. Perhaps their presence, good thoughts and prayers can be the support the close family and relatives need?

The question is often asked whether there is a difference if the ashes are placed in an urn in the ground, or are spread out over a wider area. A consideration that may be helpful in making a decision is whether it is desirable that the ashes have a focal point. In a few years the urn decomposes and the ashes will slowly spread, from the focal point, outwards.

Doing things the way you know is good

> The average man does not exist. Everyone knows it, and first and foremost the statisticians. Yet it is on this non-man that we lavish the greater part of our care and attention. The other man, the one who is capable of change, the one who could not bear it if he were to discover that he was the average, the one who only says "I know" when it is really he who knows — that man suffocates.[2]
>
> Jacques Lussyran (1924–71)

It is most important to feel free in forming the time after a loved one has died and do what we find right and good.

A family who wished to arrange most of the practical work themselves after the father of the died, described their experience:

> Father felt unwell and went to the doctors. He died there. The doctor had already made contact with the funeral directors, who had already prepared the body

and placed it in a coffin before we heard of his death. Otherwise we would have wished to care for his body ourselves. We asked the funeral directors to drive the coffin home to us. Then we thanked them and said that we would manage the rest ourselves.

For us it was important for the mourning process that we had the possibility to help.

For three days our father lay in the open coffin at home in his room. His wife for more than fifty years read from the gospel of St John for him. Father was a very special man, the mainstay of the family. We had luckily told him that while he lived. We cried much while we prepared for the burial. But these preparations were the last thing we could do for him, and therefore it was important that we could be active in this work.

We made wreaths with flowers from our own garden, as father died in the summer. One daughter made contact with the chapel authorities and rented the chapel. At the same time she arranged for the urn to be placed in the ground later. For a gravestone the family chose a beautiful stone which they found at their cottage in the countryside. Another daughter carved the wooden cross for the grave. A son in law drove the hearse with the coffin to the chapel.

We have arranged baptisms, confirmations and large weddings — why should we not also arrange the funeral when our dear father died? Today we have often become strangers to death. We shove it to one side. It has become a matter of course that the funeral directors take over. Why should the funeral directors have a monopoly at the end of life? For us it was right and important to choose differently.

Perhaps it can be a possibility for others. We have probably saved a good deal of money, but most important for us was that we could take a worthy farewell.[3]

Sister Frances Dominica established Helen House in Oxford, England as a source of practical help to children with terminal and life-threatening conditions and their families. In the introduction to her book, *Just My Reflection; Helping Parents to do Things their Way when their Child Dies,* Sister Frances Dominica described an experience:

> Before Helen House opened I met a little girl who had cancer. She and her mother and her brother lived in a small flat in our town and I got to know them well in the last six months of the child's life. Her mother determined that she would care for her daughter in her own home, once it was recognized that she would not recover. I lived with them during the last few days of the little girl's life and through the days which followed until the funeral. The mother, who was Irish, had not lost touch with her instinct to do things the way she knew was right. I stayed with her and marvelled. I learned more in those few days than I had throughout my nursing career.
>
> No doctor, nurse, pastor or funeral director was going to deter this woman from keeping her child's body at home in her bedroom until the funeral. It was she who washed and dressed the little one after death, she who brushed her hair and arranged toys and flowers around her and went in and out of the room so naturally in the days which followed. It was the mother who lifted her daughter's body into the coffin on the day of the funeral and ensured that everything was as it should be for the next stage in the child's journey. In a devastatingly imperfect world everything was as perfect as it could be.[4]

Memorial gatherings

It can often be good, after the burial, to meet. After such an important event it can be good to "come down to earth again" by sharing a simple meal. At the same time it is a good opportunity to tell of experiences with the dead one and to tell about events in his life.

A memorial gathering, held at the end of the three days or some time later, may be a good time to talk, tell more about a person's life. Many can speak and the picture, which emerges, has many aspects. It may be good to bear in mind that also for the deceased it is important how we on earth have experienced his life. In the gospel of Luke is related how the Christ walked with two disciples on the road to Emmaus, after His Resurrection. He asked them what they were speaking about. They had not recognized him and said that he must be the only one in Jerusalem who did not know what had happened. Then they relate in detail what has happened. It is conceivable that the Resurrected Christ also needed to hear from men on earth what had happened to him, as He did not know how it was experienced by human beings.

In the Christian Community, as well as in other churches, it is possible to hold a memorial service for a person who has died, offering prayers to help the one who has died on their further path.

5. Nature's Response to Human Death

Can a death have an effect on nature? Are the phenomena observed in nature after a death, connected with the death? Selma Lagerlöf's observations of nature, as she travelled to her mother's funeral, made her receptive at the funeral, she relates, for more than meets the eye. In 1936, in the first of many drafts of her short story *The Soul*, Selma Lagerlöf (1858–1940) describes her own experiences at her mother's funeral in 1915:

> I really should not doubt that there is a life after this one ... because I once experienced something very strange.
>
> You see — it happened at my mother's funeral. It took place in the church of Östra Ämtervik at the usual time after the church service. The coffin was out in the quire, covered in flowers, two servers stood motionless on both sides, and the parson had already begun his opening address. I sat and listened; it was a good speech and I took in every word. You must understand that everything was as right as it could be; we had engaged a choir from Sunne, they had sung a few songs, our nearest relations had come to the funeral and the church was full of people — of course there was nothing unusual in that, everything was simple as is the way in a small country church.
>
> We had decorated with fir branches, nothing else was to be had as Mother had died in December shortly before Christmas. Besides it was terribly cold. The

thermometer was showing twenty-four below freezing
when we sat down in the sledges. Of course we still
kept to a walking pace. I myself did not notice the
cold, but the others must have suffered from it. All the
flowers that had been laid on the coffin had turned
stiff and black on the way ...

Then I tried in every way I could to make everything as solemn, as ceremonial as possible, but what
was to be done in the cold of winter? But I should not
speak ill of the bitter cold that came so suddenly on
the day of the funeral. I don't know if I have ever seen
a more beautiful day. There was no frost on the trees,
but they were hung with drops of ice, which glistened
like a chandelier. The sun shone from a clear blue sky
and everywhere my gaze fell on white birch trees all
covered in long icicles, which glittered like sparks of
fire. I felt nature was celebrating my old mother. This
soothed my pain somewhat.

I also observed something else on the way to
church. When I came down to Lake Fryken I saw there
were swans in a bay that was not frozen over. This
may be nothing unusual, but I had never seen swans
on that lake. And I felt once more that nature wanted
to honour my mother. This was a comfort to me.

It may be that all this stirred me more than usual,
woke something within me, made me over-sensitive.

And now in the church, in the middle of the parson's address, I suddenly felt that my mother was
near me. She had come in through a window on my
right, flown up to me, and now hovered by my right
shoulder, close to my ear.

I did not see her, she was not something physical,
she was not even a translucent being of mist. She was
nothing. And at the same time I said to myself: It's
my imagination.

Yet I sensed what she wanted to tell me. That she
was happy to be released from the heavy earthly body.

That she was overjoyed to be a spirit, to be held down no longer.

This lasted only a few moments. Then she flew on, out through the left wall, and it seemed as if I was able to follow her journey over the land, swift and joyful, until she disappeared behind the hills. I drew myself up. I, too, was full of joy. Sorrow and grief were taken from me. O Mother, Mother!

A few moments later the parson's address came to an end and the thought went through my head that I should stand up and let all the people know what I had just experienced. But I was held back by the thought that, After all, I could not be quite sure. I had seen nothing, heard nothing. It could have been mere imagination, a trick of fancy.

And yet, to this day I have no hesitation in saying it is true. My mother had understood how unhappy I was and she wanted to comfort me. And for that I thank her.[1]

Butterflies and bees

A two year old girl drowned in Esbo, a town near Helsinki in Finland. It was August. At her burial the procession walked from the chapel to the grave, a path of three to four hundred meters. The caretaker walked in front with the wagon and the little coffin, the mother and the father next to the coffin, on each side. The other people walked behind the coffin.

One of the relatives noticed that a dark butterfly came flying and alighted on the coffin and was there perhaps for a minute, while the procession moved forwards, for then to fly on its way again.

During the burial service at the graveside, some raindrops fell on the mourners, even though nobody could see clouds in the sky.[2]

A man lived out in the country in Norway. He looked after his animals, especially the bees, with great love. When working with the bees he did not need any protective garments, he just was very careful so as not to harm any bee.

Time passed by, and he died. The funeral was at the local church. When the ceremony in the church was concluded, and the coffin was being carried out, they saw a swarm of bees hanging over the door of the church. All who walked under the bees had to bow their head. His daughter thought: That was the bees' farewell.[3]

Rainbows and storms

From my own experience I can relate two incidents.

A much loved music teacher in Oslo died at the age of forty-eight. His urn was placed in a country cemetery. Those gathered there started to sing a song he had composed. It started to rain, and the umbrellas came up. The graveyard sloped, and far below was the Oslo Fjord. While the song was carried by the wind, a wonderful rainbow stood above the fjord for a few moments.

Life had not been so good to a woman who had died some days before. But just in the last seven years, since she had moved and opened an alternative therapeutic practice, life had improved. Although she was already ill with, she had redecorated her dwelling and practice, preparing for the future. That autumn it had been raining most of the time. Reflecting on her life on the train journey to the funeral, the thought came that even though her life had been difficult, the sun did shine for her in her last years. Just then the sun broke through the clouds. On arriving at the crematorium, a beautiful rainbow bowed itself over the building where her body lay.

Jonathan Reid described the death of John Allan, who had lived many years in Botton Village in Yorkshire, England:

> The news of his death came as a huge shock. But within minutes of the phone call from the hospital, the weather underwent a rapid and dramatic change: purple and yellow clouds massed overhead, huge hailstones came bouncing down, and then a resplendent double rainbow appeared over the dale. People poured outside to see it. It was a display of symphonic proportions, which I felt convinced John was orchestrating.[4]

Hans Schauder's funeral left a deep impression on many:

> On the day of his funeral in Edinburgh the weather was sunny and warm. As the congregation were filing out of the chapel at the crematorium, a fairly loud rumble of thunder could be heard, quite unexpectedly. A short while later a second rumble, a little gentler, and then a still gentler third rumble. One of those present wondered if the rumbles of thunder were asking: "Have you recognized the greatness of this man?"[5]

Birds

Hildegard Hofmann of Würzburg related the following experience:

> My uncle kept pigeons as a hobby. He always cared for his birds with very much love. Sadly, he suffered a heart attack while he was quite young. The family mourned his passing very much. In the trouble we experienced, no one had given thought to the pigeons. When my uncle was to be brought to the cemetery from his house, an unforgettable sight presented itself

in the room where he lay. Around his deathbed sat the
pigeons who had gained entry through an open window. They remained silently and almost motionless
with the dead as if conducting a watch.[6]

Irene Johanson describes her experience while celebrating a
Memorial Service in the Christian Community in Munich:

A distinguished curative educationalist [Alex Baum]
died unexpectedly while on a lecture tour in Germany
... in November ... and nature was going through its
winter withdrawal. As part of the service for the dead
I gave an address. I took the name of the deceased as
an image of his being. He had been like a great tree
that had spread its branches over all Europe. Many
birds had built their nests in this tree and received
protection, nourishment, help and understanding
there. As I spoke of the tree and the birds, a chorus of
birdsong began outside in the garden. At my amen it
stopped. The whole of the large congregation had
heard it and felt it to be a confirmation of my description of this personality.[7]

Signs

Res Fischer, a leading Opera singer, describes her experiences
when Emil Bock died on December 6 and after his funeral on
December 9, 1959:

A day becomes a memorable day because of a great
event or a profound experience of the soul. Such a day
has its own light. Who has not experienced a day in
spring when the flowers blossomed more radiantly or
whose anguish or pain has turned the world colourless?
    The experience of light is of a different kind. It is
no projection of a subjective feeling, but it descended

on us from heavenly heights and determined our inner
attitude.

It was on December 6, 1959 in the morning. The
leaden, lowering sky of the preceding days was torn
open with dramatic force and the dark wall of clouds
was as if shredded and dispersed. The intensity of
light, which flooded down from the south-west, was
so extraordinary that it could not be mistaken for a
meteorological high or a sign of changing weather. It
was amazing to watch how the painfully white bright-
ness spread wider and wider.

Suddenly the constricting sorrow was transformed
into a feeling of heaven-wide freedom. A winging,
surging liberation flowed from the clarity of light and
turned the pain into deepest gratitude.

A light-blue sky, across it were racing white cumu-
lus clouds of summer density. They pile themselves
together and bank up only to vanish in the path of
wind and sun, to be piled up towerlike in the thundery
Northeast.

Everyone who walked along the Haussmann
Strasse in Stuttgart on December 9 between eleven
and twelve o'clock on his way to the church of the
Christian Community, will have been struck by this
tumult of clouds, by this tremendous movement. One
hour after this, following the first part of the funeral
service for Emil Bock the sky had become peaceful. An
extraordinary sign in the sky caught the eye. A gigan-
tic triangle stood high above the horizon in strange,
piercing tranquillity. The geometrical figure in the sky
was surprising. How did such a contradictory cloud
formation come about?

Many little fluffy-white, half-oval, light and lofty
cloud vessels freely rose diagonally upwards. The opposite side was marked by clear, hard straight lines in
short sections. Both the slanting sides of the triangle
were separating from a small bank of clouds. The blue

in the centre of the triangle, which was forming,
appeared darker. One could easily wonder if one saw the
"Eye of God" here as it is found in ancient pictures.[8]

Heinrich Hardt (1891–1981) was a young doctor working at
the Lauenstein, the first curative home, when Rudolf Steiner
died. He described his experiences as he stood outside the
crematorium:

> Beneath a cloudless, radiant spring sky a vast number
> of people had gathered outside the crematorium in
> Basle which was packed with people inside.
>   The music by Stuten has sounded and ebbed away
> and Albert Steffen's address could only be heard in
> parts by those standing outside in nature. I was filled
> with deep sorrow about the passing of our beloved
> teacher, at the imminent disappearance of his faithful
> earthly figure, the head permeated by the spirit, the
> nobility of his starry forehead. All this would now be
> surrendered to the elements.
>   Various memories — of his revelations and inti-
> mate directions regarding the whole of nature, plants,
> animals and elemental beings — passed through my
> soul. With all the dignity and beauty of the event
> which had been imparted to human hearts and hands
> I had the following feeling: it cannot be other than
> nature itself will express its participation in this hour.
> The beings of nature which were intimate brothers to
> our teacher of the spiritual world would have to show
> their taking part and their visible presence. Otherwise
> this unique, sorrowful yet sublime hour would remain
> incomplete.
>   On the gable of the grey crematorium one could see
> the shape of a large antique amphora and I was look-
> ing towards this with searching and expectant gaze:
> when and whence will come the great beautiful bird
> which will light upon it, notwithstanding the proxim-

ity of so many people? Would it show its presence in this way? However, the vase remained as it had been.

But wait — it may have been two or three minutes later when my gaze was drawn to the sky by the soft cries of seagulls and by a very gentle rushing sound. What did I see?

Directly above the crematorium at the height of about 40 metres there stood a formation like a living crown. It was formed by twenty-two or twenty-four seagulls circling eurythmically in an anti-clockwise direction. Their flight was joyful and buoyant, their plumage sparkled silvery against the brilliant light-blue sky. Their breasts were tinted with gold. This was an indescribable triad of colours. From time to time some of the birds winged through the circle in a half figure-of-eight and rejoined the circle in a new place. This crowning wreath stayed like an all-encircling corona for some minutes at exactly the same place as if held there by the hands of gods.

I nudged the friend on my right side and we looked up for a long time, gripped in our innermost being. Looking at the people around us confirmed that, sadly, nobody else was looking up. I was itching to call, to poke someone to make him aware. Alas we were still so young! The risk of disturbance made us remain silent.

Very gradually this "wedding flight," as ornithologists call this event, hovered slowly to the right and behind, always maintaining its circle. From the direction they were going the sunlight was flashing, undisturbed by any clouds! Our eyes had to close when this winged, mobile and living crown came too close to the sun's blinding rays.

Stirred in our innermost being by the beauty of this event which came as a fulfilment and touched the soul deeply, we left this place together with the others, gazed upon the silently flowing Rhine and thanked

those birds for their incredible roundelay which arose
as if from a secret connectedness.[9]

While the physical body is given to the earth, the life body or
ether body, which has harboured the experiences of the life, is
freed. These experiences appear when the life body loosens
from the physical body, as the panorama after death. The life
body can be seen as a second corpse, and spreads out, meeting the etheric in the world. Does this meeting bring about the
change in weather, and is it sensed by butterflies, bees and
birds?

6. When Death Evokes Questions

Death almost always comes as a surprise, even if we have been expecting it. The surprise, the shock, is so much greater when the death is sudden, without any warning sign. Death due to suicide, to euthanasia, violent and accidental deaths, as well as mass deaths evoke questions.

Suicide

> What do you want to do? Do you want to throw away your life? You can't do that! You can throw away your body, but nothing else![1]
>
> Quoted by Friedrich Rittelmeyer (1872–1938)

When a person dies and the cause appears to be suicide, it is important to ponder if there is really another, deeper cause. It can happen that a person takes their own life during a spell of mental illness. The death can then be seen as caused by the illness and not as suicide.

Hjalmar Gullberg (1898–1961), the Swedish poet, sets suicide in a larger perspective when he reflected over the death of his poet friend, Karin Boye, by her own hand:

It is difficult to get to the truth. Why did Karin Boye that April evening walk quietly up a hill and sit there alone under the stars, while we heard on the radio that the police in Alingås asked for help to find her? The only provisions on her last journey were sleeping pills and a bottle of water. There will be many rumours. It will be pointed to conflicts in her life or unknown sides of her being will be unearthed. One will try to come to clarity about that which actually does not concern us: another person's ultimate decision concerning themselves. The one will find this, the other that. Explanations are not hard to find. But the truth? Our ultimate actions are like a poet's poems; they have their clear motives and course, but their deepest source in our being, their most inner truth, we can only divine.[2]

Suicide is tragic, puzzling, and difficult to fathom. When a person dies a natural death, the soul will be prepared to leave the body. Even with a sudden death the shock over being separated from the body will not be as great as with a suicide. The soul of one who has taken their own life can sometimes be experienced as seeking to find its way back to the body. With this in mind, it can be worth considering burial rather than cremation, as the form of the body is preserved longer and perhaps lessens the shock of separation.

When a person talks of themselves, they often refer to their physical body. This gives the feeling of a certain experience of self. The more bound to the sense world and to their body a person is, the stronger will be this feeling of self. By taking their own life they choose to do without their body. They take away from themselves the physical basis for their feeling of self. This feeling lives on, however, in the soul together with all the needs that belong to life on earth. This may lead to painful experiences. The soul feels empty. The feeling can be compared to that of hunger and thirst, without being able to eat and drink.

The experience may be likened to a door closing behind you, without the possibility of opening it.

Suicide is no solution for problems. On the contrary, the problems are transferred to another plane of existence.

Those who are left behind can often struggle with feelings of guilt — "what could I have done differently?" A great sorrow accompanies a suicide; there is a great pain that no hand was stretched out in time. But we must know that what has happened is the deceased's own deed, fully and wholly.

Rudolf Steiner spoke clearly about suicide:

> When death comes naturally, the three bodies [physical, etheric, and astral] separate relatively easily. Even in apoplexy or any sudden but natural form of death, the separation of these higher members has in fact been prepared for well in advance, and so they separate easily and the sense of loss of the physical body is only slight. But when the separation is as sudden and violent as it is with the suicide, whose whole organism is still healthy and firmly bound together, then immediately after death he feels the loss of the physical body very keenly and this causes terrible pains. This is a ghastly fate: the suicide feels as though he had been plucked out of himself, and he begin a fearful search for the physical body of which he was so suddenly deprived. Nothing else bears comparison with this. You may retort that the suicide who is weary of life no longer has any interest in it; otherwise he would not have killed himself. But that is a delusion, for it is precisely the suicide who wants too much from life. Because it has ceased to satisfy his desire for pleasure, or perhaps because some change of circumstances has involved him in a loss, he takes refuge in death. And that is why his feeling of deprivation when he finds himself without a body is unspeakably severe.[3]

For one who has taken their own life, it is important that those left behind follow with their thoughts, love and prayers. Those who have taken their own life need our help. It may be helpful to image the dead one surrounded by light. It may be good to read the Gospel of Easter Sunday (Mark 16) which tells of the empty grave and the resurrected Christ. The verse, given by Rudolf Steiner to a mother for her son who took his life, directs the soul to Christ as mediator and helper. See the verse, "O Soul in the Land of Soul," page 121.

Especially for younger people, the experience of the one who has taken his own life can be too strong. Then it is best to set aside a time each day to quietly give the help we manage to give.

Euthanasia

> *Do not seek death. Death will find you.*
> *But seek the road which makes death a fulfilment.*[4]
>
> Dag Hammarskjöld

In her autobiography Elisabeth Kübler-Ross has described how her mother, a healthy seventy-seven year old, quite unexpectedly said:

> You are the only doctor in the family and if there is an emergency I will count on you ... If I ever become a vegetable, I want you to terminate my life.

Elisabeth Kübler-Ross finally managed to say to her mother that she was against euthanasia and would never — never ever — assist anyone:

> If something happens, I will do the same for you that I do for all my patients, I will help you live until you die.

Three days later her mother suffered a massive stroke:

> Unable to speak, she stared at me with a hundred words in her deep, injured, pained and frightened eyes. They added up to one plea, which I understood. But I knew then — as I'd known before — that I could never be an instrument of her death ...

For some reason, God saw fit to keep her alive like
this for four more years ...
    I knew it was not the end. My mother continued to
feel love and give love. In her own way, she was growing and learning whatever lessons she needed to learn.
Everybody should know that. Life ends when you have
learned everything you are supposed to learn. Therefore any thought of ending her life, as she had asked,
was even more unimaginable than before ...
    As long as she continued to survive without artifi-
cial life support, there was nothing to do, except to
love her.[5]

The question can be asked if there is an inner meaning in
suffering excruciating pain, in bearing a difficult life situation. Likewise in growing old, in living on when there is no
longer any outer ground for it. Everyone would have to look
at his or her life and try to answer the question themselves.
Perhaps we can discover in that which has been difficult,
much that has enhanced our lives, that has helped us to grow
as human beings. *To grow old*, means to grow while becoming old.

Through the possibility of prolonging life through life
support machines, sensitivity is needed to know when the
moment has come to turn off the machines and let nature
take its course. Someone related that his mother had been
unconscious and kept alive by life support machines, and the
doctors said there was no possibility of her recovering. The
family had asked the doctors to decide. After the machines
were switched off and she had died, the son wondered if they
had been right to leave the decision to the doctors alone —
should the family perhaps have been more involved in the
decision?

The moment of death is important, and it can happen that
the responsibility to divine the moment of death for another
individual can be placed in our hands. It is not easy to balance the possibility of life being cut off too soon, or it being

prolonged unnecessarily. To have to make a decision when the machines are to be switched off and nature left to take its course, is always a special and unique challenge. Only out of the given situation can a real decision be made. The doctors know the medical prognosis; the family are personally connected with the individual; nurses are involved both personally and objectively. Together, family, doctors and nurses can talk about the options, and allow time to let the decision ripen. Then the right moment may be found, so that later no one will ask: "Was what we did good?"

Violent deaths and accidents

You, who have gone
so suddenly,
Torn from this life:
We are still with you
As you are with us.

You, who have found
so suddenly
Light weaving of love:
We are still with you
As you are with us.

May our will guide you
In the mill of creation,
For we, who would sorrow,
Find purpose: Your light.

May our thoughts balm you
In the kiln of renewal,
For we, who would miss you,
Meet comfort: Your love.[6]

Jens-Peter Linde

Many years ago a sailor sailed westwards. The ship was on the high seas for months on end. Contact with home was minimal in the days before radio and telegraph. One night the sailor's wife had an experience of her husband. He stood there in the house, dripping wet. After a moment that seemed like an age for her, he disappeared. She wondered what the appearance could mean. Some weeks later there was a knock on the door. The local vicar had come. Before he could begin, she said: "I know." She knew that her husband was dead.

We all know that we will die, some day. The time is unknown. This does not mean that we cannot begin preparing ourselves for death. Already in the middle of life there is the possibility to begin the preparation. Older people think about death as they feel their strength ebb away. They discover signs that tell them that they are ageing. In a quiet way they prepare for the transition that death brings.

Those who are torn out of life by an accident or through a violent death will not have had this time of preparation beforehand. This may be a truth that needs modification. Pondering over a sudden death, there may be signs of inner preparation for it. Generally, a violent death or an accident will tear a person out of life. The transition will not be prepared. Can it be compared to a travel situation? When we know we will travel to another country we can prepare ourselves. We try to learn the other country's language and customs. We acclimatize culturally as much as we can and look forward to the journey. With violent or accidental death this preparation is usually not possible. Perhaps the individual, now bereft of the body, will "not know where he is." We can do what we can to help the individual find his way in the new landscape he is now in after death.

Mass death

People tend to turn their thoughts away from mass death, and this is very understandable. Everyone hears so much about death all round the world, and sees it so often on the news, that it can all

become somewhat remote. Only the individual
death of someone who is known, that is a reality.[7]

Kalmia Bittleston

Mass death may occur in natural catastrophes, major accidents, epidemics such as AIDS, and through terror and war.

Natural catastrophes, such as earthquakes and volcanic eruptions, affect a whole district, causing families, friends and neighbours to die at the same time — enabling souls who belong together on the earth to continue their way side by side, thus strengthening their perception of destiny for the future.

People killed in accidents, terror or war, have happened to come together without knowing or even wishing to know each other. By their common death they become united and have a shared destiny. They all look back on the same event. They find themselves among strangers and each will have to make an effort to connect himself again with the threads of his own destiny.

The remaining members of a family, or of a group of friends, might feel a guilt that they survived but, at the same time, they may have the feeling that it is not by chance, but that there is still something for them to do on earth. One important activity will have been the sending of shared memories and loving thoughts to those now living in spirit-heights, thus enriching their existence and maintaining the links which still bind them to the earthly life which they were forced to leave behind.

As always, when something happens, there will have been people who had extraordinary escapes. Either they were away at just that time, or they missed the train, plane, or boat. Perhaps they were protected by some freak of nature from falling walls or rising water, or their own courage and determination may have made their survival possible.[8]

7. The Death of Children

My body is just my reflection ...
When you die you leave your reflection.
Your real self leaves your body and
goes into another world ... where
it will be the happiest life of all ...
God has the answers, we have the
questions, and only in the end
will he tell us the answers.
God has kept that new life a secret
and I am glad because it will give
us a surprise, it will give us such
a big surprise.[1]

Garvan Byrne, aged 11, a year before he died

When we have done all the work we were sent to
Earth to do, we are allowed to shed our body,
which imprisons our soul like a cocoon encloses the
future butterfly.
And when the time is right, we can let go of it
and we will be free of pain, free of fears and
worries — free as a very beautiful butterfly,
returning home to God ...[2]

Elisabeth Kübler-Ross from a letter
she wrote to a child with cancer

The death of an older person can be experienced as the course of nature. It may be hard when it happens, yet usually can be accepted. The death of a child is quite different. The child is still in the coming. We find no answers from nature, a child's death is unnatural. We describe below the death of a few children. In the chapter on grief the experiences of parents when a child dies are described.

When Friedrich Rittlemeyer (1872–1938) was four he and his fifteen-month-old younger sister both had scarlet fever. Many years later he wrote:

> While my little sister was in the throes of scarlet fever I was led into a dream during the night; it was rather more than a dream. An angel entered the room through the window. He took no notice of me but went to the tiny bed of my slumbering little sister. Taking the child carefully in his arms he rose upwards with her. I see this picture in front of my soul till this day. The sickroom then returned to its dark contours. The figure appeared larger than life-size and completely irradiated by light. There were no distinct facial features but it was a being filled with quiet certainty and secret dignity.
>
> I was abruptly shocked out of my blissful visions by the lamentations of my mother. She had fallen asleep in total exhaustion and on waking suddenly found the dead child at her side. Without entering into her anguish I started joyfully to talk about my experience. I did not know yet what the meaning of dying is, at least what it means for men on earth. But my child-like account was like angelic balm for my mother. Had it not been meant for her also?[3]

When she was a child Elisabeth Kübler-Ross was once very ill and was taken to hospital. She described later her experience of the girl she shared a room with:

> The next thing I remember is waking up in a strange room. It was actually more like a glass cage. Or a fish bowl ...
>
> There was another bed in the fishbowl. It was occupied by a little girl who was two years older than I. She was very frail and her skin was so pale and sickly it appeared to be translucent. She reminded me

of an angel without wings, a little porcelain angel. No
one ever visited her.

She drifted in and out of consciousness, so we
never actually spoke. But we were very comfortable
with each other, relaxed and familiar. We stared into
each other's eyes for immeasurable periods of time. It
was our way of communicating ...

Then one day, shortly before my own illness took a
drastic turn, I opened my eyes from a dreamy sleep and
saw my room-mate looking at me, waiting. We then
had a beautiful, very moving and purposeful discus-
sion. My little porcelain friend told me that she would
be leaving later that night. I grew concerned. "It's
okay," she said. "There are angels waiting for me."

That evening she stirred more than normal. As I
tried to get her attention, she kept looking past me, or
through me. "It's important that you keep fighting,"
she explained. "You're going to make it. You're going
to return home with your family." I was so happy, but
then my mood changed abruptly. "What about you?" I
asked.

She said that her real family was "on the other
side" and assured me that there was no need to worry.
We traded smiles before drifting back to sleep. I had
no fear of the journey my new friend was embarking
on. Nor did she. It seemed as natural as the sun going
down every night and the moon taking its place.

The next morning I noticed that my friend's bed
was empty. None of the doctors or nurses said a word
about her departure, but I smiled inside, knowing that
she had confided in me before leaving. Maybe I knew
more than they did.[4]

A little boy drowned many years ago. Looking back at the
accident his family discerned that he had unconsciously prepared for it, and wondered why everything that could have
helped him was prevented from doing so:

He was seven years old and should have begun school
that year. He went indoors and told his mother that he
wanted to go to a party and wanted to have white
clothes on. He went to the neighbour's garden and
picked a bunch of Iris flowers and took them to his
mother. He then went outside.

The small children made a canoe and he was the
one who was going to try out the canoe in the water.
It filled with water and he drowned.

The children called for help. A doctor who lived
nearby heard the call. He began to run, but between
him and the accident spot was a railway line and
just at that moment a train came. He had to wait
until the train had gone past and by then it was too
late.

The boy drowned where it was not very deep. He
could have held his head above the water but he pan-
icked and drowned. When the ambulance arrived it
had new equipment which the paramedics did not
know how to operate properly.[5]

Another family were astonished that their son had been saved
after he fell head first into a deep well, with nobody nearby:

He was three years old when the following happened.
He lived on a farm in Norway. On the neighbouring
farm a gardener lived and they were good friends.
Almost every day he visited his gardener friend.

One day, when he was going to go home, his gardener friend gave him a bunch of carrots to take to his
mother. On his way he went past a well, and the
thought came that he should rinse the bunch of carrots, as they were full of earth. No sooner did he think
of this than it was done. But in doing so he fell head
first into the well, and the well was deep.

Shortly afterwards he came soaking wet, happy
and satisfied, and gave the carrots to his mother with

greetings from the gardener. His mother was very
shocked, — he was soaking wet.

"What has happened?" she asked.

"I fell into the well — I was going to rinse the
carrots."

"But how did you get up again?"

"An angel came and pulled me up," he answered.

It did not seem as if he was in the least afraid or
frightened by the experience.[6]

For those nearest a child who has died, for the grieving parents, there are many questions. Why did the child die? Outer
reasons will be found but are there deeper grounds? Was a
death from an accident already being prepared for, in some
way, already beforehand? Can the boy who wished to have his
best clothes on the day he drowned have had a premonition of
his death? A three-year-old child drowned in Brazil in February 1983. The mother had a premonition some months before:

Nothing I could have done would have prevented the
events that lay ahead of my daughter and myself that
day, which I truly believe to be our fate. Call it destiny
if you prefer, perhaps karma, give it whatever term
you like, but it was meant to happen the way it happened, and at that precise period in my life.

I know, too, that I was given a warning of these
events some months prior to the accident. It was
sometime before the Christmas of 1982 when I had
the strangest of dreams. As it turned out, the dream
was to become an actual living nightmare.

In my dream I saw one of my children falling into a
swimming-pool. The child was wearing very little,
except for shorts or something similar. When Lisa
drowned, due to the hot weather, she was just wearing
a swimsuit.

In my dream, at the place where the child fell into
the pool, there were railings very similar to those on

our own balcony. Susan's house [where the child drowned], too, had an upstairs area with railings and, of course, the swimming-pool in the front garden.

This dream upset me so much that I told another friend, Anita, about it. Now I am very glad I did tell someone before the accident happened.

My mother often says: "What is for you will not go past you," meaning that we cannot avoid our fate whatever it may be. My life seemed to lead up to that day, February 7, 1983, and the way it has continued makes me believe that nothing could have stopped the events of that day occurring.[7]

Burial for children

In the Christian Community there is a burial service for children who die before the age of Confirmation (about fourteen years of age), and another for those over this age. This is an acknowledgment that death is basically different for a child. In the funeral service for children in the Christian Community the ritual words speak of the child as not having walked their own way on earth. Only at the age of Confirmation does the young person begin to go their own way, to begin living their individual biography.

We do not lose children who die

Rudolf Steiner often spoke during the First World War about the dead and our connection with them. Once he spoke of the difference in this connection with those who die as children and as adults:

Now it is not at all the same when a soul passes through the gate of death in relatively early years or later in life. The death of young children who have loved us, is a very different thing from the death of people older than ourselves. Experience of the spiritual world discovers that the secret of communion with children who have died can be expressed by saying that in the spiritual sense we do not lose them, they remain with us. When children die in early life they continue to be with us — spiritually with us. I should like to give to you as a theme for meditation, that when little children die they are not lost to us; we do not lose them, they stay with us spiritually. Of older people who die, the opposite may be said. Those who are older do not lose us. *We* do not lose little children: elderly people do not lose *us*. When elderly people die they are strongly drawn to the spiritual world, but this also gives them the power so to work into the physical world that it is easier for them to approach us. True, they withdraw much farther from the physical world than do children who remain near us, but they are endowed with higher faculties of perception than children who die young. Knowledge of different souls in the spiritual world reveals that those who died in old age are able to enter easily into souls on earth; they do not lose the souls on earth. And we do not lose little children, for they remain more or less within the sphere of earthly man ...

The same distinction holds good for all our thoughts about those who have died. It is best for a child when we induce a mood of feeling connected with him, we try to turn our thoughts to him and these thoughts will draw near to him when we sleep. Such thoughts may be of a more general kind — such for example as may be directed to all those who have passed through the gate of death. In the case of an elderly person, we must direct our thoughts of remembrance to him as an individual, thinking about his life on earth and of the experiences we shared with him. In order to establish the right intercourse with an

older person it is very important to visualize him as
he actually was, to make his being come to life in ourselves — not only by remembering things he said
which meant a great deal to us but by thinking of
what he was as an individual and what his value was
for the world. If we make these things inwardly alive,
they will enable us to come into connection with an
older person who has died and to have the right
thoughts of remembrance for him. So you see, for the
unfolding of true piety it is important to know what
attitude should be taken to those who have died in
childhood and to those who have died in the later
years of life.[8]

8. Grief

Believe, when you are most unhappy, that there is
something for you to do in the world. So long as
you can sweeten another's pain, life is not in
vain.[1]

Helen Keller (1880–1968)

When his wife died, the writer C.S. Lewis (1898–1963) noted his experience of grief, day by day. Although grief is experienced very individually, it may be of help to others to ponder over a few of his observations:

No one has ever told me that grief felt so like fear. I am not afraid, but the sensation is like being afraid. The same fluttering in the stomach, the same restlessness ...
   There is a sort of invisible blanket between the world and me. I find it hard to take in what anyone says. Or perhaps, hard to want to take it in. It is so uninteresting. Yet I want the others to be about me. I dread the moments when the house is empty. If only they would talk to one another and not to me ...
   There are moments, most unexpectedly, when something inside me tries to assure me that I don't really mind so much, not so very much, after all. Love is not the whole of a man's life ...
   Then comes a sudden jab of red-hot memory and all this "commonsense" vanishes like an ant in the mouth of a furnace.
   On the rebound one passes into tears and pathos. Maudlin tears. I almost prefer the moments of agony.

These are at least clean and honest ...

And no one ever told me about the laziness of grief. Except my job — where the machine seems to run on much as usual — I loathe the slightest effort. Not only writing but even reading a letter is too much. Even shaving. What does it matter now whether my cheek is rough or smooth? ...

I do not only live each endless day in grief, but live each day thinking about living each day in grief ...

I see people, as they approach me, trying to make up their minds whether they'll "say something about it" or not. I hate it if they do, and if they don't ...

It is hard to have patience with people who say "There is no death" or "Death doesn't matter." There is death. And whatever is matters. And whatever happens has consequences, and it and they are irrevocable and irreversible ...

Something quite unexpectedly has happened. It came this morning early. For various reasons, not in themselves at all mysterious, my heart was lighter than it has been for many weeks. For one thing, I suppose I am recovering physically from a good deal of mere exhaustion ... And suddenly at the very moment when, so far, I mourned H. least, I remembered her best. Indeed, it was something (almost) better than memory; an instantaneous, unanswerable impression. To say it was like a meeting would be going too far. Yet there was that in it which tempts one to use those words. It was as if the lifting of the sorrow removed a barrier.

Once very near the end I said, "If you can — if it is allowed — come to me when I too am on my death bed."

"Allowed!" she said. "Heaven would have a job to hold me; and as for Hell, I'd break it into bits." She knew she was speaking a kind of mythological language, with even an element of comedy in it. There was a twinkle as well as a tear in her eye. But there was no myth and no joke about the will, deeper than any feeling, that flashed through her.[2]

Sorrow can be felt as pain, often as physical pain. It may take time to accustom oneself to that. We do not need to be strong the whole time. We may have the need to talk about the deceased time and again. Our friends can help just by listening. As a physical sore needs time to heal, so our grief must take its time — often many, many years. Especially when we have lived together for many years, we have grown together in the sphere of life — do not those who have been married for a long time even begin to resemble one another? The pain of being separated is real, here and now. As time passes, perhaps moments of joy will come again; it may be longer between the hard times, even though they will return — at festive times, birthdays, Christmas, at weekends, or small events that bring the loved one to mind.

A man often spoke with his family that he hoped that no one would hold him back when he died. Nobody knew then that he had cancer and would die within a year. For his family it was a task not to wish him back, but to live on in thankfulness for what he had been in life.

Many people experience anger in their grief. They can be angry, often over small things. It is good to be clear that this is a normal reaction.

Even through the hardest blow of destiny we will be able to experience peace of soul if we try to look back in thankfulness, and try to meet that what comes to us with an open mind. As Dag Hammarskjöld noted for himself:

> Night is drawing nigh —
> For all that has been — Thanks!
> To all that shall be — Yes!

> Will it come, or will it not,
> The day when the joy becomes great,
> The day when the grief becomes small?
> (Gunnar Ekelöf)

It *did* come — the day when the grief became small.
For what had befallen me and seemed so hard to bear
became insignificant in the light of the demands
which God was now making. But how difficult it is to
feel that this was also, and for that very reason, the
day when the joy became great.[3]

Grief when a child dies

> *The life she did not live, has become our inner life.*
>   Father of a child who died at birth.

A mother whose thirteen-year-old daughter was killed in a
road accident described three years later her experience of her
grief:

> Very few of my many good friends, from near and far,
> were able to give me any real help. Lots of love and
> sympathy, and many kind thoughts, reached me, but
> they helped little. No one seemed able to really grasp
> or *feel* what had happened. The finality was over-
> whelming.[4]

The mother of the three-year-old who drowned in Brazil says
it this way:

> Unless you too are a bereaved parent then you should
> be careful about how you offer advice to grieving par-
> ents, who are very vulnerable. If you are not sure
> what to say, it is safer not to say anything. Just offer
> to be with them, allow them to talk, especially about
> their child ...
>   When the initial shock begins to subside, all that is
> left is the pain.
>   The pain endured as bereaved parents is very tangi-
> ble. It is like no other pain ever experienced before. It

cannot be seen by anyone, and this seems odd, because for the suffering parent it surrounds every minute of their life. They have lost a vital part of their body, but no one except them knows how real the loss is ...

What society does not realize is that for bereaved parents, it is after the first six or seven weeks that the first waves of shock start to lift, when the real agony truly begins ...

From here on, life is an unrelenting pilgrimage through pain and turmoil. For instead of being able to accept what has happened and get on with their lives, they wake up to the reality that their child can no longer be part of that future they are expecting to face ...

Yes, life does go on, but the pain of the loss goes on too ...

My main two pieces of advice which are worth repeating, that I give to newly bereaved parents are: first, trust your gut instincts. If it seems the right thing to do, then do it. Second, take one day at a time — do not look forward until you are ready to do so.[5]

Rudolf Steiner described the intrinsic difference in the grief we feel when a child dies and an adult dies:

When little children have died, the pain of those who have remained behind is really a kind of compassion — no matter whether such children were their own or other children whom they loved. Children remain with us and because we have been united with them they convey their pain to our souls; we feel their pain — that they would fain still be here! Their pain is eased when we bear it with them. The child feels in us, shares his feeling with us, and it is good that it should be so; his pain is thereby ameliorated.

On the other hand, the pain we feel at the death of elderly people — whether relatives or friends — can be called egotistical pain. An elderly person who has died does not lose us and the feeling he has is therefore different from the feeling present in a child. One who dies in later life does not lose us. We here in life feel that we have lost him — the pain is therefore *ours;* it is egotistical pain. We do not share his feeling as we do in the case of children; we feel the pain for ourselves.

A clear distinction can therefore be made between these two forms of pain: egotistical pain in connection with the elderly; pain fraught with compassion in connection with little children. The child lives on in us and we actually feel what he feels. In reality, our own soul mourns only for those who died in the later years of their life.[6]

9. A Bridge from Soul to Soul

*There is a land of the living and a land of the dead,
and the bridge is love, the only survival, the only
meaning.*[1]

Thornton Wilder (1897–1975)

Paul McCartney's mother, Mary, died in 1956 when he was
fourteen years old. In 1968 he wrote the song *Let it Be:*

> When I find myself in times of trouble
> Mother Mary comes to me
> Speaking words of wisdom,
> Let it be.
>
> And in my hours of darkness
> She is standing right in front of me
> Speaking words of wisdom
> Let it be ...[2]

Letter from William Blake (1757–1827) to William Hayley
Esq., dated Lambeth May 6, 1800:

> Dear Sir,
> I am very sorry for your immense loss, which is a
> repetition of what all feel in this valley of misery &
> happiness mixed . . I know that our deceased friends
> are more really with us than when they were appar-
> ent to our mortal part. Thirteen years ago, I lost a
> brother & with his spirit I converse daily and hourly
> in the Spirit, and See him in my remembrance in the
> regions of my imagination. I hear his advice & even

now write from his Dictate — Forgive me for expressing to you my Enthusiasm which I wish all to partake
of Since it is to me a Source of Immortal Joy even in
this world; by it I am the companion of Angels. May
you continue to be so more & more & to be more
and more persuaded, that every Mortal loss is an
Immortal Gain. The Ruins of Time build Mansions in
Eternity ... Feeling heartily your Grief with a brother's
Sympathy
 I remain Dear Sir Your humble Servant
  WILLIAM BLAKE[3]

In a legend of the Scolt Lapps a grandmother tells her grand-
son about the Northern Lights and the dead:

When the leaves of the trees begin to turn yellow in
the Autumn, it is because they're going to die. And the
souls of human beings do the same thing. They
become brighter as death comes nearer. But instead of
falling as the leaves do, they fly away right up into
the sky. As long as they were on the earth and hidden
by the body, one could not see them clearly, but up in
the sky there is nothing that hides them.

When the shadows of winter lie on the earth the
souls of the dead come too and show themselves to
the living, so that they may have patience and
courage enough to wait for the return of the Spring
and the sun. From one end of the sky to the other the
souls dance in the Northern Lights, and give us a
much better light than the moon or the stars."

"Grandmother," cried Mika, whose face was all lit
up by the gleam from outside, "when you are dead
will you dance up there with the others?" Mika could
not keep from smiling a little at the idea of grandmother dancing.

"I don't know, dear, whether they want me up
there."

"And will you make little signs to me out of the sky?"

"No, Mika, for you will not be able to recognize me. But I shall recognize you, and if you think about me very nicely and very often I shall perhaps be able to give you a little help on your path. You see there are countries that have not so long winter as ours. They have no need of the Northern Lights, but their dead are around them just the same and will protect them if they call to them. Only one must pray a great deal for the dead, and above all must never, never think of them as lying in their coffins under the earth. When you see someone bathing you don't go and talk to the clothes that he has left behind on the bank.[4]

Selma Lagerlöf and the dead

One looks on life not much differently when one grows old.
Just one thing changes: The dead are so near.
One confides in them. One converses more with them than with the living.[5]

Selma Lagerlöf (1858–1940) August 20, 1939

In 1930 Selma Lagerlöf received a letter from Holland.[6] The writer asked Selma Lagerlöf for advice how she could thank a dead person for saving her life. Selma Lagerlöf took a year before she answered the letter. By that time she had lost the address of the woman in Holland, so both her answer and the original letter were found after her death in 1940 amongst the thousands of letters she had stored throughout her life.

The writer of the original letter was married to a doctor. They lived in a small town in Holland together with their five small children. Due to an influenza epidemic the husband was overworked, and she worried for his health. A doctor

friend advised them to move out into the country, for his
sake. Unexpectedly, a letter came from the head of a sanato-
rium in the countryside. He wrote that his wife had died, and
that it was lonely for him out there. He offered the post to the
woman's husband. The doctor wanted to decline the post, but
his wife telegraphed their acceptance.

After a time there she became ill. Also, the children
became pale and had stomach-ache.

The woman now began to write about the supernatural.
The first time she had come to the house she had suddenly
seen a hearse standing in front of the house. The horses
scraped with their hooves, but when she came near they had
disappeared. She asked an old gardener what was the cause
of the doctor's wife's death. He told her that all was well, she
was very kind, but had had stomach-ache and had died.

After a while they all became ill. The doctor tried to find
the cause, but found nothing. She thought they would all die
but then the children recovered. Some friends came to visit.
They took a walk on the nearby heath. The men walked in
front, the women followed. Suddenly a third woman was with
them. Her friend did not seem to see this other woman. She
thought about the hearse. The figure walked the whole time
next to her and as long as she was there the impression she
gave was that she wanted to say something. Suddenly she
realized with a shock that it was the dead woman, and that
she was trying to warn her. She told her husband about the
experience that evening, but he thought it too fantastic.

Some days later she woke in the middle of the night
because someone seemed to push her. She sat up in the bed
and saw, in a corner of the bedroom, the same figure she had
seen on the heath. The expression in her face was such that
it was clear she wanted to say something. The woman spoke
to the figure, said she was not afraid, and asked if she was
the doctor's wife who had died, perhaps of the same illness
which she and her family suffered from, and if she should
continue the search for the cause. The expression in the figure's face relaxed and she disappeared.

The next morning the woman asked her husband to send samples once again to a laboratory. He did it for her sake and that same evening a telegram came which said that white lead was found in the sample. Investigation showed that the water cistern had been painted with paint containing lead and together with the acids in the water had formed a poison. If this had not been discovered, all the family would have been dead within months.

It took the woman five years to recover. The figure never returned. She had saved them all. And now the she asked Selma Lagerlöf if she knew how she could thank the dead woman.

Selma Lagerlöf did not know. But she thought a lot about it. A year later a thought came to her and she replied:

Mårbacka, Sunne, Sweden 18.3.1931
You have not forgotten I suppose the long letter you wrote to me more than a year ago about the dead woman who had so kindly and miraculously come to your help, and that you asked me if I could tell you any way to give her a sign of your gratitude.

I have not answered that letter. It interested me very much, and I have often thought of it, but it was a somewhat strange question and I did not know how to answer it.

But today an idea has come to me, and I will tell you a very plain story out of my own life.

As you perhaps know, I live far away in the country at the same place as my father and his father lived. My parents and grandfather and grandmother and other relations have their burial place in the churchyard of this parish, all at the same spot. But on this burial place, there has never been any monument neither a cross, nor even a simple stone with their names, nothing but a rosebush in the midst and a hedge about the whole. I really don't know why it was so plain, but it had always been so.

Well, when I bought back my parental home in
1910, and when I came to live here, my first thought
was to put a fine monument on the grave of my fore-
fathers, but that thought was not realized before last
year. You see, I wished to have a *beautiful* monument,
and I did not know what to chose as best. I saw many
churchyards, but the many different things that were
put up at the graves did not please me. And I was not
rich, I had to build so many new houses on my farm
and so many old ones needed restoring, and I had so
many, many young people among my relatives to help
with their studies, and the dead at the churchyard had
to wait. But my conscience was troubled, and so I had
an architect to give me a design and last summer it
was all finished.

You ask me in your letter if I can believe you, now I
must ask you if you can believe me.

I must tell you that while I have been very happy
in my authorship I have had much trouble in my private life; it has not been easy at all. Economic trou-
bles among other things which I need not go into. But
this autumn and even this new year things have been
much better. This morning while lying in bed I
reflected on how much better things had become compared to previous years, and while pondering this I
thought of my dead and I asked myself if it was they
who had helped me now in gratitude for the monument on their grave. You must not laugh, but you cannot know how many questions have been resolved,
how many things that have gone wrong for years,
suddenly have begun to alter. It is most curious
indeed. And so I resolved to write to you, that there
could be a possibility that the dead like to have their
names remembered by us who live. No one knows, but
it is a possibility.

If you could put up somewhere on your hospital a
table of names of the predecessors of your husband

with their wives or acknowledge them in some other manner? I send back your letter. Who knows in what hands it might fall after my death? I should be thankful if you would return my own,
Yours very truly
Selma Lagerlöf.[7]

Selma Lagerlöf continued living with the questions posed by the woman's letter. During the ten years until she died in 1940, Selma Lagerlöf tried many times to write a short story about life after death. She tried many approaches, and after her death one ot the attempts, *The Soul,* was published. In *The Soul* many of the elements from the woman's original letter are incorporated.

In one of the drafts, probably from about 1936, Selma Lägerlöf includes a letter in her short story where the questions she was to live with for her remaining years are asked:

Is it possible to come in contact with the dead?
Can one give the dead signs of one's thankfulness?

Our relationship with the dead

Rudolf Steiner related an experience he had as a boy. He was sitting alone in the waiting room of the railway station where his father worked. The door opened, and a woman came in. She stopped and said: "Try now and in the future to help me as much as you can." After a while she disappeared and the boy was alone.

Later it became known that at exactly the time the woman had appeared to the boy, a near relative had taken her own life.[8]

Through his perception of the spiritual world, Rudolf Steiner could help many who had lost someone close.

Your relationship with the Dead must be one of the

heart, of inner interest. You must remind yourself of
your love for the person when he was alive and
address yourself to him with real warmth of heart,
not abstractly. This feeling can take such firm root in
the soul that in the evening, at the moment of going
to sleep, it becomes a question to the Dead without
your knowing it. Or you may try to realise vividly
what was the nature of your particular interest in the
one who has died. Think about your experience with
him; visualize actual moments when you were
together with him, and then ask yourself: What was
it about him that particularly interested me, that
attracted me to him? When was it that I was so
deeply impressed, liked what he said, found it helpful
and valuable? If you remind yourself of moments
when you were strongly connected with the Dead and
were deeply interested in him, and then turn this into
a desire to speak to him, to say something to him —
if you develop the feeling with purity of heart and let
the question arise out of the interest you took in him,
then the question of the communication remains in
your soul, and when you go to sleep it passes over to
him.[8]

When loved ones pass over into the other worlds, it is
vitally important that we send them our thoughts and
feelings, without allowing the thought to arise that
we wish to have them back. The latter makes existence in the sphere into which they must pass more
difficult for the departed. We should send the *love*
that we give them — and not the *pain* that we feel —
into the worlds where they are. Do not misunderstand
me; we should not become hardened or indifferent.
Yet it ought to be possible for us to view the dead
with the thought, *"May my love go with you! You are
surrounded by it."* To my knowledge, a feeling such
as this is like a winged garment that carried loved

ones upward, whereas the feelings of many people when they mourn — which we may express as "Ah, if only you were still with us" — become an obstacle to them.

The above is a *general* indication of how we should compose our feelings when a loved one has left us.[9]

10. The Further Path
of the Soul

The body of
B. Franklin,
Printer;
Like the Cover of an old Book,
Its Contents torn out,
And stript of its Lettering and Gilding,
Lies here, Food for Worms.
But the Work shall not be wholly lost:
For it will, as he believ'd appear once more,
In a new and more perfect Edition,
Corrected and amended
By the Author.[1]

Benjamin Franklin (1706–90)

Benjamin Franklin explained his views thus:

When I see nothing annihilated [in the works of God] and not a drop of water wasted, I cannot suspect the annihilation of souls, or believe that He will suffer the daily waste of millions of minds ready made that now exist, and put Himself to the continual trouble of making new ones. Thus, finding myself to exist in the world, I believe I shall, in some shape or other, always exist; and, with all the inconveniences human life is liable to, I shall not object to a new edition of mine, hoping, however, that the *errata* of the last may be corrected.[2]

Rudolf Steiner described the path of the soul after death.

Here we continue his description after the physical body, the first corpse, and the life body (etheric body), the second corpse, have been discarded, as described above:

> If we can clearly envisage what will remain when we are parted from all our physical organs, from everything that normally fills our daytime consciousness and enlivens our soul, from everything for which we have to be grateful to the body all day long, we shall begin to form some conception of what the condition of life is after death, when the two corpses have been laid aside. This condition is called Kamaloka, the place of desires. It is not some region set apart. Kamaloka is where we are, and the spirits of the dead are always hovering around us, but they are inaccessible to our physical senses. What, then, does a dead man feel? To take a simple example, suppose a man eats avidly and enjoys his food ... Now suppose a man dies: what is left to him is his desire and capacity for enjoyment. To the physical part of a man belongs only the means of enjoyment: thus we need gums and so forth in order to eat. The pleasure and the desire belong to the soul, and they survive after death. But the man no longer has any means of satisfying his desires, for the appropriate organs are absent. And this applies to all kinds of wishes and desires. He may want to look at some beautiful arrangements of colours — but he lacks eyes; or listen to some harmonious music — but he lacks ears.
> How does the soul experience all this after death? The soul is like a wanderer in the desert, suffering from a burning thirst and looking for some spring at which to quench it; and the soul has to suffer this burning thirst because it has no organ or instrument for satisfying it. It has to feel deprived of everything, so that to call this condition one of burning thirst is appropriate. This is the essence of Kamaloka. The soul

is not tortured from outside, but has to suffer the torment of the desires it still has but cannot satisfy.

Why does the soul have to endure this torment?
The reason is that man has to wean himself gradually
from these physical wishes and desires, so that the
soul may free itself from the Earth, may purify and
cleanse itself. When that is achieved, the Kamaloka
period comes to an end ...

How does the soul pass through its life in
Kamaloka? In Kamaloka a man lives through his
whole life again, but backwards. He goes through it,
day by day, with all its experiences, events and
actions, back from the moment of death to that of
birth. What is the point of this? The point is that he
has to pause at every event and learn how to wean
himself from his dependence on the physical and
material. He also relives everything he enjoyed in his
earthly life, but in such a way that he has to do without all this; it offers him no satisfaction. And so he
gradually learns to disengage himself from physical
life. And when he has lived through his life right back
to the day of his birth, he can, in the words of the
Bible, enter into the "kingdom of Heaven" ...

How long does a man remain in Kamaloka? For
about one-third of the length of his past life. If for
instance he has lived for seventy-five years, his time
in Kamaloka will be twenty-five years ...

When a man has lived through his time in
Kamaloka, he is ready to raise the higher part of his
astral body, the outcome of his own endeavours, and
to leave the lower part behind . . . The remaining part
is the third human corpse, consisting of the lower
impulses and desires which have not been transmuted.[3]

The life body (etheric body) loosens during the three days
after death. It is then discarded as the second corpse. The

time in Kamaloka is the time we have slept in life, approximately one third of the length of our life on earth. Then the third corpse is discarded, and the essence of our experiences on earth is taken further.

Reincarnation

In many parts of the world reincarnation is accepted as part of life. In the western world this is not so, yet there are many who experience reincarnation as a reality:

> I feel in myself the future life. I am like a forest once cut down; the new shoots are stronger and livelier than ever ... You say the soul is nothing but the resultant of the bodily powers? Why, then, is my soul more luminous when my bodily powers begin to fail? The nearer I approach the end the plainer I hear around me the immortal symphonies of the worlds which invite me. It is marvellous yet simple. It is a fairy tale and it is history.
>
> For half a century I have been writing my thoughts in prose and in verse; history, philosophy, drama, romance, tradition, satire, ode and song; I have tried all. But I feel I have not said a thousandth part of what is in me. When I go down to the grave I can say like many others "I have finished my day's work," but I can not say, "I have finished my life." My day's work will begin again the next morning. The tomb is not a blind alley; it is a thoroughfare. It closes on the twilight. It opens on the dawn.[4]
>
> Victor Hugo (1802–85)

> We wake and find ourselves on a stair; there are other stairs below us which we seem to have ascended; there are stairs above us, many a one, which go upward and out of sight. But the Genius which

according to the old belief stands at the door by which
we enter, and gives us the lethe to drink, that we may
tell no tales, mixed the cup too strongly, and we cannot shake off the lethargy now at noon day. Sleep
lingers all our lifetime about our eyes.[5]

Ralph Waldo Emerson (1803–82)

We all return; it is this certainty that gives meaning to
life and it does not make the slightest difference
whether or not in a later incarnation we remember the
former life. What counts is not the individual and his
comfort, but the great aspiration to the perfect and the
pure which goes on in each incarnation.[6]

Gustav Mahler (1860–1911)

The more I observe and study things, the more convinced I become that sorrow over separation and
death is perhaps the greatest delusion. To realize that
it is a delusion is to become free. There is no death,
no separation of the substance. And yet the tragedy of
it is that though we love friends for the substance we
recognize in them, we deplore the destruction of the
insubstantial that covers the substance for the time
being. Whereas real friendship should be used to
reach the whole through the fragment. You seem to
have got the truth for the moment. Let it abide
forever ...

What you say about rebirth is sound. It is nature's
kindness that we do not remember past births. Where
is the good either of knowing in detail the numberless
births we have gone through? Life would be a burden
if we carried such a tremendous load of memories. A
wise man deliberately forgets many things, even as a
lawyer forgets the cases and their details as soon as
they are disposed of. Yes, "death is but a sleep and a
forgetting."[7]

Mohandas K. Gandhi (1869–1948)

Pre-existence is a reality on which the existence of the soul is founded. Here we must balance the purely egoistic conception of the soul's post-existence — which springs only from our desire to continue living after death — with knowledge of the soul's pre-existence. We must lift ourselves again to a perception of the true eternity of the soul, but in a different way than before ...[8]

Rudolf Steiner (1861–1925)

Poetry

the lesson of falling leaves

the leaves believe
such letting go is love
such love is faith
such faith is grace
such grace is god
i agree with the leaves

Lucille Clifton

The Last Invocation

At the last, tenderly,
From the walls of the powerful fortress'd house,
From the clasp of knitted locks, from the keep of well-
    closed doors,
Let me be wafted.

Let me glide noiselessly forth;
With the key of softness unlock the locks — with a
    whisper,
Set ope the doors O soul.

Tenderly — be not impatient,
(Strong is your hold O mortal flesh.
Strong is your hold O love.)

Walt Whitman

As I Watch'd the Ploughman Ploughing

As I watch'd the ploughman ploughing,
Or the sower sowing in the fields, or the harvester
    harvesting,
I saw there too, O life and death, your analogies;
(Life, life is the tillage, and Death is the harvest
    according.)

Walt Whitman

Pensive and Faltering

Pensive and faltering,
The words *the Dead* I write,
For living are the Dead, (Haply the only living, only
    real,
And I the apparition, I the spectre.)

Walt Whitman

The Swan

This clumsy living that moves lumbering
as if in ropes through what is not done
reminds us of the awkward way the swan walks.

And to die, which is a letting go
of the ground we stand on and cling to every day,
is like the swan when he nervously lets himself down

into the water, which receives him gaily
and which flows joyfully under
and after him, wave after wave,
while the swan, unmoving and marvelously calm,
is pleased to be carried, each minute more fully grown,
more like a king, composed, farther and farther on.

Rainer Maria Rilke
Translated by Robert Bly

A Journey Ends

I have seen death too often to believe in death.
It is not an ending...but a withdrawal,

    As one who finishes a long journey,
    Stills the motor,
    Turns off the lights,
    Steps from his car
And walks up the path
To the home that awaits him.

Don Blanding

Crossing the Bar

Sunset and evening star,
    And one clear call for me!
And may there be no moaning of the bar,
    When I put out to sea,

Be such a tide as moving seems asleep,
    Too full for sound and foam,
When that which drew from out the boundless deep
    Turns again home.

Twilight and evening bell,
    And after that the dark!
And may there be no sadness of farewell,
    When I embark;

For tho' from out our bourne of Time and Place
    The flood may bear me far,
I hope to see my Pilot face to face
    When I have crost the bar.

Alfred, Lord Tennyson

Death is a Dialogue between
The Spirit and the Dust.
"Dissolve," says Death. The Spirit, "Sir,
I have another Trust."

Death doubts it — Argues from the Ground.
The Spirit turns away,
Just laying off, for evidence,
An Overcoat of Clay.

Emily Dickinson

Death stand above me, whispering low
I know not what into my ear:
Of his strange language all I know
Is, there is not a word of fear.

Walter Savage Landor

After death

"What does it feel like when one grows wings, when
   one is dead, mother?"
"First your back bends, it grows broad and great.

Then it grows heavier and heavier. It is as if one carried a mountain.
There is a shaking and breaking in ribs and backbone
   and marrow.

Then it straightens up with a jerk and bears all, all.
Then one knows that one is dead now and lives in a
   new form."

Karin Boye
Translated by David McDuff

There is No Death

There is no death! The stars go down
    To rise upon some other shore,
And bright in heaven's jeweled crown
    They shine for evermore.

There is no death! the dust we tread
    Still change beneath the summer showers
To golden grain, or mellow fruit,
    Or rainbow-tinted flowers.

There is no death! An angel form
    Walks o'er the earth with silent tread;
He bears our best loved ones away,
    And then we call them dead.

Born unto that undying life,
    They leave us but to come again;
With joy we welcome them—the same
    Except in sin and pain.

And ever near us, though unseen
    The dear immortal spirits tread;
For all the boundless universe
    Is life—there are no dead!

John Luckey McCreery

The Existence of Love

I had thought that your death
Was a waste and a destruction,
A pain of grief hardly to be endured.
I am only beginning to learn
That your life was a gift and a growing
And a loving left with me.
That desperation of death
Destroyed the existence of love,
But the fact of death
Cannot destroy what has been given.
I am learning to look at your life again
Instead of your death and your departing.

Marjorie Pizer

I am The Gentle Autumn Rain

Do not stand at my grave and weep
I am not there. I do not sleep.
I am a thousand winds that blow
I am the diamond glints on snow.
I am the sunlight on ripened grain
I am the gentle autumn rain.
When you awaken in the morning's hush,
I am the swift uplifting rush
Of quiet birds in circling light.
I am the soft stars that shine at night.
Do not stand at my grave and cry,
I am not there; I did not die.

Anon

We'll meet again

They say you will not come again,
    but I shall always hear your voice
    in silence and in song,
    and feel you ever near.

They say that you have passed beyond,
    unto the joy supreme,
    but I can always call you back
    into the land of dream.

For death is but a gateway
    to the great reality,
    a new beginning,
    not an end of human destiny.

For love is all,
    and life goes on in spite of grief and pain,
    and deep within my heart I know
    that we shall meet again.

                                        Anon

I am there

Look for me when the tide is high
And the gulls are wheeling overhead
When the autumn wind sweeps the cloudy sky
And one by one the leaves are shed
Look for me when the trees are bare
And the stars are bright in the frosty sky
When the morning mist hangs on the air
And shorter darker days pass by.

I am there, where the river flows
And salmon leap in the silver Lune
Where the insects hum & the tall grass grows
And sunlight warms the afternoon
I am there in the busy street
I take your hand in the city square
In the market place where the people meet
In your quiet room — I am there.

I am the love you cannot see
And all I ask is — look for me.

Iris Hesselden

Though I am dead
grieve not for me with tears,
Think not of death
with sorrowing and fears;
I am so near that
every tear you shed,
Touches me although
you think me dead.
But when you laugh
and sing in glad delight,
My soul is lifted
upwards to the height,
Laugh and be glad
for all that life is giving,
And I, though dead,
will share your joy in living.

Anon

I call your name

I call your name,
But if you should reply
How shall I know your voice
In sound of wind and wave,
In sea-bird's cry?

Or if from sleep
Some image rise
Though angel-bright, how know
Among the mingling currents of the dreaming deep
It tells of you?

Or does my doubt impede
Those messengers
Whose footsteps everywhere always come and go,
The world a single thought
Wherein the one love seeks, and in a thousand ways,
Answering, the one love replies.

Kathleen Raine

To —

Music, when soft voices die,
Vibrates in the memory —
Odours, when sweet violets sicken,
Live within the sense they quicken.

Rose leaves, when the rose is dead,
Are heaped for the beloved's bed;
And so thy thoughts, when thou art gone,
Love itself shall slumber on.

Percy Bysshe Shelley

A Creed

I hold that when a person dies
    His soul returns again to earth;
Arrayed in some new flesh-disguise
    Another mother gives him birth.
With sturdier limbs and brighter brain
The old soul takes the road again.

Such is my own belief and trust;
    This hand, this hand that holds the pen,
Has many a hundred times been dust
    And turned, as dust, to dust again;
These eyes of mine have blinked and shone
In Thebes, in Troy, in Babylon.

All that I rightly think or do,
    Or make, or spoil, or bless, or blast,
Is curse or blessing justly due
    For sloth or effort in the past.
My life's a statement of the sum
Of vice indulged, or overcome.

I know that in my lives to be
    My sorry heart will ache and burn,
And worship, unavailingly,
    The woman whom I used to spurn,
And shake to see another have
The love I spurned, the love she gave.

And I shall know, in angry words,
    In gibes, and mocks, and many a tear,
A carrion flock of homing-birds,
    The gibes and scorns I uttered here.
The brave word that I failed to speak
Will brand me dastard on the cheek.

And as I wander on the roads
    I shall be helped and healed and blessed;
Dear words shall cheer and be as goads
    To urge to heights before unguessed.
My road shall be the road I made;
All that I gave shall be repaid.

So shall I fight, so shall I tread,
    In this long war beneath the stars;
So shall I faint and show the scars,
Until this case, this clogging mould,
Be smithied all to kingly gold.

John Masefield

We Are Seven

— A simple Child,
That lightly draws its breath,
And feels its life in every limb,
What should it know of death?

I met a little cottage Girl:
She was eight years old, she said;
Her hair was thick with many a curl
That clustered round her head.

She had a rustic, woodland air,
And she was wildly clad:
Her eyes were fair, and very fair;
— Her beauty made me glad.

"Sisters and brothers, little Maid,
How many may you be?"
"How many? Seven in all," she said,
And wondering looked at me.

"And where are they? I pray you tell."
She answered, "Seven are we;
And two of us at Conway dwell,
And two are gone to sea.

"Two of us in the church-yard lie,
My sister and my brother;
And, in the church-yard cottage, I
Dwell near them with my mother."

"You say that two at Conway dwell,
And two are gone to sea,
Yet ye are seven! I pray you tell,
 Sweet Maid, how this may be."

Then did the little Maid reply,
"Seven boys and girls are we;
Two of us in the church-yard lie,
Beneath the church-yard tree."

"You run about, my little Maid,
Your limbs they are alive;
If two are in the church-yard laid,
Then ye are only five."

"Their graves are green, they may be seen,"
The little Maid replied,
"Twelve steps or more from my mother's door,
And they are side by side.

"My stockings there I often knit,
My kerchief there I hem;
And there upon the ground I sit,
And sing a song for them.

"And often after sun-set, Sir,
When it is light and fair,
I take my little porringer,
And eat my supper there.

"The first that died was sister Jane;
In bed she moaning lay.
Till God released her of her pain;
And then she went away.

"So in the church-yard she was laid;
And, when the grass was dry,
Together round her grave we played,
My brother John and I.

"And when the ground was white with snow,
And I could run and slide,
My brother John was forced to go,
And he lies by her side."

"How many are you, then," said I,
"If they two are in heaven?"
Quick was the little Maid's reply,
"O Master! we are seven."

"But they are dead; those two are dead!
Their spirits are in heaven!"
'Twas throwing words away; for still
The little Maid would have her will,
And said, "Nay, we are seven!"

William Wordsworth

"We are seven" was first published in *Lyrical Ballads* (1798). In the preface
to the 1802 edition Wordsworth described the poem as dealing with "the
perplexity and obscurity which in childhood attend our notion of death, or
rather our utter inability to admit that notion."[1]

Ode: Intimations of Immortality
from recollections of Early Childhood

The Child is Father of the Man;
And I could wish my days to be
Bound each to each by natural piety.

I
There was a time when meadow, grove, and stream,
The earth, and every common sight,
        To me did seem
        Apparelled in celestial light,
The glory and the freshness of a dream.
It is not now as it hath been of yore; —
        Turn wheresoe'er I may,
        By night or day,
The things which I have seen I now can see no
        more ...

V
Our birth is but a sleep and a forgetting;
The Soul that rises with us, our life's Star,
        Hath had elsewhere its setting,
        And cometh from afar.
        Not in entire forgetfulness
        And not in utter nakedness
But trailing clouds of glory do we come
        From God, who is our home:
Heaven lies about us in our infancy!
Shades of the prison-house begin to close
        Upon the growing Boy;
        But He
Beholds the light, and whence it flows,

He sees it in his joy;
The Youth, who daily farther from the east
     Must travel, still is Nature's Priest,
     And by the vision splendid
     Is on his way attended;
At length the man perceives it die away
And fade into the light of common day . . .

William Wordsworth

First published in 1807. Wordsworth wrote in a note to this ode: "Nothing was more difficult for me in childhood than to admit the notion of death as a state applicable to my own being. I have said elsewhere —

A simple child,
That lightly draws its breath,
And feels its life in every limb,
What should it know of death!" —

But it was not so much from (feelings) of animal vivacity that *my* difficulty came as from a sense of the indomitableness of the spirit within me."
     Christopher Wordsworth observed further:
     "In my 'Ode on the Intimations of Immortality in Childhood,' I do profess to give a literal representation of the state of the affections and of the moral being in childhood. I record my own feelings at the time — my absolute spirituality, my 'all-soulness,' if I may so speak. At the time I could not believe that I should lie down quietly in the grave, and that my body would moulder into dust."[2]
     In a letter to Mrs Clarkson (January 1815), William Wordsworth further observed of the ode:
     "This poem rests entirely upon two recollections of childhood, one that of a splendour in the objects of sense which is passed away, and the other an indisposition to bend to the law of death, as applying to our particular case. A Reader who has not a vivid recollection of these feelings having existed in his mind cannot understand that poem."[3]

Verses and Prayers given by Rudolf Steiner

Prayer during illness

Spirit of God,
Fill Thou me,
Fill me in my soul.
To my soul give strength,
Strength also to my heart,
My heart that seeks for Thee,
Seeks Thee with earnest longing,
Longing to be whole and well,
Whole and well and full of courage,
Courage the gift from the hand of God,
Gift from Thee, O Spirit of God.
Spirit of God,
Fill Thou me.

Meditative prayer to find inner peace

Quiet I bear within me.
I bear within myself
Forces to make me strong.
Now will I be imbued
With their glowing warmth.
Now will I fill myself
With my own will's resolve.
And I will feel the quiet
Pouring through all my being.
When by my steadfast striving
I become strong
To find within myself
The source of strength,
The strength of inner quiet.

Prayer to be prayed for one who is very ill
To be used during a crisis and not by the person who is ill

Hearts that love, suns that warm
Ye footprints of Christ in the Father's world-all.
We call you out of our own hearts
We seek you in our own spirit
    O strive to him/her.

Rays of the human hearts, warm, mindful, longing,
Ye home-lands of Christ, in the Father's house of
    earth,
We call you out of our own hearts
We seek you in our own spirit
    O live with him/her.

Radiant love of man, warming glow of the sun,
Ye soul-vestments of Christ, in the Father's temple of
    man:
We call you out of our own hearts
We seek you in our own spirit
    O help in him/her.

For after the wake

This verse can be used to close a memorial evening held for one who has died. After the human relationships on earth have been spoken about, the realm of the angels is called upon and taken in.

Angels, Archangels and Archai
in the Ether weaving,
receive man's web of Destiny.

In Exusiai, Dynamis and Kyriotetes,
in the astral feeling of the Cosmos,
the just consequences of the earthly life of man
    die into the realm of Being.

In Thrones and Cherubim and Seraphim,
as Their Deeds of Being,
the justly transmuted fruits of the earthly life of man
    are resurrected.

George Adams, who translated these words into English, noted:
"In the lectures in which these sentences were given, Rudolf Steiner described how in the three successive stages of the life after death the spiritual Hierarchies progressively receive and transmute the fruits of man's earthly life. Expressing it in these meditative sayings, he recommended the practice of thinking thus concretely about the Dead. "We utter a simple and good, a wonderful and beautiful prayer, when we think of the connection of life and death, or of one who has passed through the gate of death, in this way. Much depends upon it, whether human beings on earth *think* the spiritual facts or not: whether they merely accompany the Dead with thoughts that remain behind on earth, or accompany them on their further path with thoughts that are a true image of what takes place in yonder realm which they have entered ... Therefore human hearts should be ready to hear once more, what human hearts *did* hear in the Mysteries and Initiation-centres of olden time when they called out impressively, again and again to those who were about to be initiated: 'Accompany the Dead in their further Destinies!'"

The three sentences may also be spoken or meditated on behalf of an individual soul. Then the words "man's web of destiny" can be replaced by "thy web of destiny," and the words "the earthly life of man" by "thy earthly life,"—or the name of the departed may be inserted."[1]

For one who has died

May my soul's love *strive* to you
May my love's meaning *stream* to you.
May they *bear* you
May they *hold* you
In the heights of *hope*,
In the spheres of *love*.

For one who has died

Upwards to thee strive the love of my soul,
Upwards to thee flow the stream of my love!
    May they sustain thee,
    May they enfold thee
    In heights of Hope,
    In spheres of Love.

For one who has died

May my heart's warm life
Stream to your soul,
To warm your coldness
To soothe your heat.
May *my* thoughts live in *your* thoughts—
And your thoughts in my thoughts—
In the spiritual worlds.

Rudolf Steiner wrote to Paula Stryczek on the death of a dear friend and explained the meaning of coldness and heat in the verses for the dead:

"It is important that you have the right feeling towards the words 'warmth' and 'coldness.' Physical 'warmth' and 'coldness' are not what is meant, but something like 'warmth of feeling' and 'coldness of feeling,' through it is not at all easy for a person clothed in a physical body to have any idea of what these qualities mean to a disembodied soul. Such souls have to become aware that the astral body, which they still have around them, is effective, though it cannot make use of the physical organs. Much of what human beings strive for here on earth is given by our physical organs, which are no longer there. This lack of the physical organs is similar — but only *similar* — to a feeling of burning thirst transferred onto the soul. There are the strong feelings of 'burning thirst' experienced after a person has left the body. And it is just the same with what the will desires to do. The will is accustomed to using the physical organs, but it no longer has them. This 'privation' approximates to a feeling of coldness in the soul. It is precisely with regard to these feelings that the living can help the so-called dead; for these feelings do not *merely* result from a person's individual life, but are connected to the mysteries of incarnation. It is thus possible to aid someone who has died ..."

For a child who has died

To you
In love
On Christ's Ways
Seek my heart
Live
in my thoughts
As I live in your soul.

For one who has committed suicide

O Soul in the land of soul
Seek Christ's grace
That brings you aid,
Aid from spirit lands,
And gives peace
To those spirits
Who, experiencing no peace,
Want to despair.

The Lord's Prayer Prayed with the Dead

by Rudolf Frieling

Our Father, who art in the Heavens,
Hallowed be thy name.
Thy Kingdom come,
Thy will be done,
 as above in the Heavens,
 so also on the earth
Give us this day our daily bread,
And forgive us our trespasses,
 as we forgive those who trespass against us.
Lead us not into temptation,
But deliver us from the evil.
 For thine is the kingdom,
 The power and the glory,
 For ever and ever,
  Amen.

When praying the words of "Our Father" we are united through the "our" with those who have died. Once we become aware of this, then we will notice how, in the whole text of the prayer, in all its requests, certain overtones and undertones are echoed that have their origin in this interconnection with the departed souls.

 Pondering the opening words,

Our Father who art in the heavens,

we are embraced with that same, elevated peace of the higher worlds which shines from the countenance of one who has died. It is true that the corpse is only the mortal remains, the garment of the soul, which has been laid aside. But sometimes it is as if the departing soul would throw a fleeting reflection of what it is now experiencing, onto that discarded garment. As if in that singularly solemn and lofty nature of the countenance of one who has died, the eternal world of the Father would mirror itself, the world into which the soul has entered.

And with this there is also present a reflection of mankind's eternal individuality, the ever-constant spirit-personality, which is itself one of the many stars of the Father's heavenly horizon. This "eternal star" does not only stand above the cot of a child, it also stands above a death-bed, shining as a reflection from the brow of the one who has died.

In death minor issues and events of daily life are forgotten, and that which is central, essential in the life and nature of the deceased, comes to our consciousness. We are able to view the completed biography, which only now, viewed at the culminating moment of death, becomes clear in its unique course. When we seek to recognize that which is essential and central to a person, we are in a certain sense spelling out his eternal name. The eternal name announces the being of the eternal spirit-personality, as it once lived in the consciousness of God, as it gradually should now be grasped by mankind.

When the star that approaches earth shines over the child's cot, it can be the inspiration for the parents to choose the right name. An earthly name cannot, of course, ever completely correspond to the eternal name, but it can be a more or less suitable replacement for that other name. The earthly name, when it is "right," can to some extent at least mirror its archetype. Just as the star above the cot can inspire the mystery of the name, so too can the withdrawing star above the deathbed reveal the "name" of the one who has died.

The deceased are not "dead," their path is one of mighty experiences actually leading to their coming close to a conscious grasp of their eternal "name ." When we, the bereaved, try to spell out this name, we meet with what the deceased himself is experiencing. We are able to look at their completed life together with them, and can try to recognize how, with more or less success, the language of the biography was able to write the star-name into the dust of the earth.

Just as the earthly name has its heavenly archetype in the eternal name, so does this have its divine archetype in the name of Christ. The "I-Am" which speaks in Christ is the archetype, from which our speaking the words "I am" is often far removed. In Christ's "I am" the Name of God is truly revealed. The more we learn to connect ourselves with Christ, the more our "I" will shine in the light of his "I," the more clearly our eternal being will write its name in the dust of the earth announcing itself and, at the same time, God.

We look together with the deceased at this ongoing process of development, finding ourselves united in the prayer-mood that allows our human I to come ever closer to becoming a pure servant and messenger for the "divine I." From a distance we sense what Hölderlin was trying to formulate in the mystery-words, "Names since Christ, are like the breath of morning." In this way we can pray the first petition, together with the deceased:

Hallowed be thy name.

Working out of the eternal centre of their being, the deceased has woven their particular life-tapestry. Every person is surrounded by such a tapestry which comes into being through the individual deeds and traits — something of a "life-space" which the soul creates around itself, so that one can say: everyone lives in "their own world."

But this "world of ours" is not yet the greatest or ultimate which can come into being around our "I." When the "I" is sanctified, this life-space will then become a place of divine life. For this reason destiny breaks into our life-tapestry as it is forming, to hinder — often dramatically — the premature development of an enclosed realm. It is their realm which death destroys time and again, but only with the intention of creating a higher order of life-space in which we should one day live.

When a person dies who has been close to us, we also take leave of their individual life-tapestry, their realm, in which we had also been allowed to feel at home, and which had become familiar and cherished. The greatest pain of a bereavement can be the moments where details of this terminated life-tapestry come to our consciousness, where we are painfully reminded of this or that trait or habit of the deceased's life, which is now absent.

Once again, we can join together with the deceased in taking leave of their earthly life-space, from that which had been their earthly nature, from their unique earthly being. Together with the deceased we can sense the importance of this pain which is connected to the leave-taking: the entrance of death is not harsh destruction, but a creating of space in which mankind will in future be able to build a higher life-space around itself. Looking towards this future state we can pray with the deceased

Thy Kingdom come.

With this we are already on the way to really saying "yes" to destiny. The more we understand this, the more any selfish wishes to have the deceased return to us disappear. Thus we make it easier for the deceased to free themselves from their earthly past and reach out towards new shores. Whoever rebels against the fact of a death, wishing it to be otherwise, makes it difficult for the deceased to find their way in their new existence. It helps them when we join with them to say "yes" to destiny. Then we pray with them:

Thy will be done.

Surrendering to the will of God can strengthen mankind in its active participation in bringing about the realization of this will, and not just accepting it unthinkingly. We should consciously become an active organ of this will. The additional line:

*As above in the heavens, so also on the earth
receives in this way a particular nuance: The will of God on
earth will come about through our help.*

Can we thus let the deceased pray with us? Do the affairs of
the earth still have significance for those who have embarked
on their path into the spiritual worlds? It is true that we
should not weigh them down with trivial details of earthly
events. But the larger decisions of earthly destiny also have a
meaning for the deceased. In fact, the more someone has
worked through their own affairs, and the less they are
caught up in the difficulties of their own development, the
more they have "their hands free" to send out their help from
above to those dear to them on earth. Christians of old knew
the importance of the help which shone to them from the
souls of the martyrs.

They will be done, as above in the heavens ... We are
strengthened when we place ourselves in the stream of divine
will. If we open our hearts to God and live either passively or
actively within his will we shall gain in strength, just as a
nourishing meal gives strength to the body. It is not by
chance that in the Lords Prayer we are led from divine will to
daily bread. Friedrich Rittelmeyer often pointed to the Johan-
nine words of Christ: "My nourishment is to work out of the
will of Him who sent me ..." (John 4:34 Tr. Madsen). This
nourishment is not only for those on earth, it also has meaning for those who have died.

> Such the Spirits' sustentation,
> With the freest ether blending:
> Love's eternal Revelation,
> To Beatitude ascending.
>
> *Johann Wolfgang von Goethe*
> *Translated by Bayard Taylor*

The word of Christ: "I am the bread of life" holds good for
the spiritual world too. Bread is not only for the angels

(Thomas Aquinas' *Panis Angelorum)* as in the hymn "Lo, the Angels' Food is given," (Hymn No. 521) but also for those who have died can benefit from its effect.

The fourth petition we can also pray together with those who have died.

Give us this day our daily bread.

In our wish to receive this "pure nourishment" of Christ, we become aware of our inadequacy. We feel our guilt. The petition of forgiveness follows on directly from the "daily bread."

This nourishment is also a meal of the community. The Divine Son can only nourish us with his being in as much as we do not deny our fellow human beings our attitude of love. *"As we forgive ..."*

The fifth petition always takes on a special quality when spoken at the funeral. The earthly life of the deceased can now be put to rights. They recognize clearly now all that was not right in their earthly life. They experience strongly all that they have taken on as failings. They experience this now more forcefully then they ever did on earth.

On the other hand the bereaved sometimes become more aware in the face of death how reconciliation among people is needed. Something of the delicate nature of conscience, which the deceased sense in encountering their guilt, can be felt. This often begins with the one dying. The dying can feel hopelessly laden down by guilt towards another. Receiving the forgiveness of the other truly eases the dying process.

This becomes clearest in the fifth petition when it is deepened by the inclusion of the deceased:

Forgive us our trespasses, as we forgive those who trespass against us.

In looking at guilt we become aware of our weakness which has been inherited since the Fall, since Lucifer's intervention. We seek divine guidance, divine proximity as counterbalance to the enormously threatening might of the temptation. In this way we can feel divine guidance, making it easier for it to lead us. Formulated positively the sixth petition is asking for divine proximity. Here too we find ourselves together with the deceased:

Lead us not into temptation.

The wish awakens for one's own "I" to be able to exist free of concern for the machinations of the devil. The longing tawakens to be allowed to be an "I" without falling prey to egotism awakens. Is that possible? To say "I" without egotism? Christ fulfilled it. As He spoke "I Am," the world became not darker but lighter. In his "I" the Name of God became manifest.

The seventh petition brings us again to the hallowing of the name. It is the petition for the egohood, free of egotism, for the freeing of the I from the might of evil. Buddhism speaks with the striking picture of the "knot in the heart" which must be loosened.

The star of the eternal individuality becomes visible once more.

> That all of mortality's
> Vain unrealities
> Die, and the Star above
> Beam but Eternal Love!
>
> *Johann Wolfgang von Goethe*
> *Translated by Bayard Taylor*

Formulated positively it is the petition for the fulfilment through divine love, when we pray together with the deceased:

But deliver us from the evil.

Then the closing word* of affirmation gains another quality, when in our "*Amen,*" the "*Amen,*" the "*Yea, so be it*" resound which is spoken by the deceased.[1]

---

* The last three lines of the Lord's Prayer are not in the oldest versions of the Bible, having been added later. Frieling did not write about them.

Practical details

If we are present at the moment of death, it may be good to pause, before plunging into all that needs to be seen to, and collect our thoughts. Speaking the Lord's Prayer aloud may bring peace to this important moment.

We can carefully close the eyes and place something under the chin, so the mouth is closed. If the death occurs in a hospital, there will be someone present who knows what to do.

If the death occurs at home, the dead one may need to be washed and cared for. The clothes one wishes can be put onto the deceased.

Whom to contact

Family, friends and colleagues. After we have told those who are closest, we can think if there are others — friend or colleague — whom one would like to tell.

Doctor. A doctor must write out the death certificate. If death has occurred outside a hospital a doctor must be called. It may be possible that the deceased can stay at home, or one can ask for the coffin to be brought home, if one wishes that.

Post mortem. If we does not wish for an autopsy it is important to say so as soon as possible. Often it will be no problem. The post mortem laws are different in different countries. If one does not wish to have an autopsy, it is important to investigate the law. In many countries, with a sudden death, or where the cause of death is unclear, it may be necessary for a post mortem.

Priest or minister. The priest or minister should be contacted as soon as possible if the deceased belonged to a church, or wishes for the burial to be held in a congregation. The priest or minister needs to be actively involved in conversations concerning the burial, and can give advice and help for the bereaved.

Funeral director. The funeral director should be contacted as early as possible so as to arrange the time and place of the funeral.

The funeral director can arrange whatever is needed. This can be of great help in a difficult situation. It may, nevertheless, be good to decide what is best. How would the deceased have imagined the funeral? You may wish to be involved in the practical arrangements. It may be of comfort and help in the process of mourning to be able to make things as good as possible for the dead one.

Funeral directors are experienced, give advice and answer any questions, which may arise. It is advisable to be open about any details, for example what the costs will be. How would the dead one have wished the funeral? Perhaps you have had the possibility to talk it over or perhaps details have been written down beforehand? It is always of great help for those left behind if this is done.

The funeral director can be asked for advice, about the rights of the bereaved. They will also know about any financial help for burials or transporting coffins home from abroad, which is available in some countries. Again they will be able to give information about how the death is to be registered.

Others. It may be helpful to make contact with the social services as they can advise and often have booklets which enumerate the possiblities.

Later you can contact the companies concerned about bank accounts, insurance, pension rights.

Endnotes

Introduction
1 Scott 1918. 181.

1. Approaching Death
1 Eckermann and Soret 1883. 84.
2 Hammarskjöld 1964. 63, 136.
3 This section is from Button 1971.
4 Variations on the theme of this prayer, found in many languages, indicate a common origin. Christoph Friedrich Oetinger may be the original source.
5 Button 1989. 3.
6 Falkberget 1974. 239.
7 Solzhenitsyn 1971. 232.

2. The Moment of Death
1 Steiner 1995. 125.
2 Button 1989. 5f.
3 Translated by David McDuff.
4 From "A Parable of Immortality" by Henry Jackson van Dyke. Often attributed to Victor Hugo, and said to come from "The Toilers of the Sea" (1866). The quotation cannot be found in the English translation of Hugo's book.
5 After Uthaug 1990. 127f.
6 Wolf-Gumpold 1969. 150f.
7 Kübler-Ross 1997. 41.
8 Scholl, 1966. 95.
9 Gollwitzer 1958. 81–85.
10 Koster 1993. 60–62.

3. The Three Days Following Death
1 Bock 1992. 65.
2 Button 1989. 4f.
3 Torvik 1989. 130.
4 Moody 1975. 66f, relating a near-death experience.
5 Steiner 1970. 28f.

4. The Burial
1 Dominica 1997. 82. Original source unknown.
2 Lusseyran 1999. 105 in a lecture prepared shortly before his unexpected death.
3 From an interview in *Bergens Tidende,* Bergen, Norway, October 20, 1995, with Esther Krogh Sælen and her daughter Turid B. Sveen, after Olaf Sælen had died.
4 Dominica 1997. xxi.

5. Nature's Response
1 de Vrieze 1976. 17-19. Translated from the Swedish by Barbro and Timothy Edwards.
2 Related by Lars-Åke Karlsson.
3 Related by Liv Holtsmark.
4 *Botton Highlights.* December 2001.
5 Schauder & Franke. 2002. 169.
6 Bock 2002. 14.
7 Johanson 2002. 41.
8 *Die Christengemeinschaft,* May 1960. 155f. Translated by Friedwart Bock.
9 Bock 2002. 14.

6. When Death Evokes Questions
1 *Die Christengemeinschaft.*
   August 1930. 140. Advice to a
   farmer who wanted to commit
   suicide.
2 Boye 1942. 5. Introduction.
3 Steiner 1970. 32.
4 Hammarskjöld 1964. 136.
5 Kübler-Ross 1997. 158–62.
6 Unpublished. August 31, 1997.
7 Bittleston 1983. 2.
8 This section is adapted from
   Bittleston 1983. 2.

7. The Death of Children
1 Dominica 1997, at the beginning of the book.
2 Kübler-Ross 1997, at the beginning of the book.
3 Rittelmeyer 1937. 12, translated by Friedwart Bock.
4 Kübler-Ross 1997. 30f.
5 Related by Nina Gramstad.
6 Related by Maren Myren.
7 Madil 2001. 21f.
8 Steiner 1985. 24f & 27f.

8. Grief
1 Watson 1988. 123.
2 Lewis 1966. 5–7, 11, 15, 38f,
   63.
3 Hammarskjöld 1964. 87.
4 von Schilling 1988. ix.
5 Madil 2001. 30–32, 49.
6 Steiner 1985. 26.

9. A Bridge from Soul to Soul
1 Wilder 1947, concluding words.
2 Lennon & McCartney 1987.
   259–63.
3 Blake 1988. 705.

4 Crottet 1949. 80f.
5 De Vrieze 1976. 34.
6 De Vrieze 1976. 3–16.
7 Steiner 1948. 10f.
8 Steiner 1985. 22f.
9 Steiner 1999. 229, from a letter
   to Paula Stryczek, Berlin Dec
   31, 1905.

10. The Further Path of the Soul
1 Labaree 1959. 109–11.
2 Head & Cranston 1985. 233.
3 Steiner 1970. 30–34 from the
   lecture held on August 24,
   1906: "The Life of the Soul in
   Kamaloka."
4 Head & Cranston 1985. 206.
5 Head & Cranston 1985. 237.
6 Spect 1925. 55.
7 Head & Cranston 1985. 10.
   Quoting Wordsworth's "Intimations of Immortality" (see p.
   112).
8 Steiner 1994. 185. From a lecture November 30, 1919.

Poetry
1 Wordsworth 1977. 947.
2 Wordsworth, C. *Memoirs II.*
   476.
3 Wordsworth 1977. 978f.

Verses by Rudolf Steiner
1 From George Adams's notes in
   Steiner 1961 p. 236f.
2 Steiner 1999. 230.

The Lord's Prayer
1 *Die Christengemeinschaft,*
   March 1940. Translated by Mal-
   colm Allsop.

Sources

Poetry

Anon. "I am The Gentle Autumn Rain." The poem was found in the pack of Lance Bombadier Stephen Cummings after he was killed by the IRA and became widely known through this event. Stephen Cummings' father read the poem on the BBC and tens of thousands requested a copy. The press also mentioned that these words were found among Marilyn Monroe's papers years earlier. (Information from Friedwart Bock)

Anon. "We'll meet again." During the Normandy invasion in 1944 a piece of paper was picked up from the battlefield, on which these lines were written.

Anon. "When I am dead." Spoken at a funeral. Source unknown.

Blanding, Don (1894–1957). 1943. *Pilot Bails Out.* New York. Dodd, Mead & Co.

Boye, Karin (1900–1941). 1994. *Complete Poems*. Tr. from Swedish by David McDuff. Newcastle upon Tyne. Bloodaxe. (Reprinted by kind permission of the translator.)

Clifton, Lucille (born 1936). 1987. *Good Woman: Poems and a Memoir 1969–80*. New York. BOA Editions. (Reprinted by kind permission of the publisher.)

Dickinson, Emily (1830–86). 1975. *The Complete Poems*. ed. Thomas H. Johnson. London. Faber.

Hesselden, Iris (born 1929). No date. "Only a Whisper Away." Morecambe, Privately printed. (Reprinted by kind permission of the author.)

Jennings, Elizabeth (1926–2001). 1986. *Collected Poems 1953–85*. Manchester. Carcanet. (Reprinted by permission of the publisher.)

Landor, Walter Savage (1775–1864). 1936. *The Complete Works of Walter Savage Landor.* London. Chapman & Hall.

Linde, Jens-Peter (born 1950). (Unpublished poem reprinted by kind permission of the author.)

Masefield, John (1878–1967). 1910. *Ballads and Poems.*
(Reprinted by permission of the Society of Authors.)

McCreery, John Luckey (1835–1906). "There is No Death."

Pizer, Marjorie. 1981. *To You the Living, Poems of Bereavement and Loss.* Sydney. Pinchgut. (Reprinted by permission of the author.)

Raine, Kathleen (born 1908). 1977. *The Oval Portrait and other poems.* London. Hamish Hamilton. (Reprinted by kind permission of the author.)

Rilke, R.M. (1875–1926). 1981. *Selected Poems.* New York. Harper & Row.

Shelley, Percy Bysshe (1792–1822). 1958. *The Golden Treasury of Songs and Lyrics.* Comp. Francis Turner Palgrave. London. Dent.

Tennyson, Alfred, Lord (1809–83). 1958. *The Golden Treasury of Songs and Lyrics.* Comp. Francis Turner Palgrave. London. Dent.

Whitman, Walt (1819–92). 1986. *The Complete Poems.* London. Penguin.

Wordsworth, William (1770–1850). 1977. *The Poems.* London. Penguin.

Verses and Prayers by Rudolf Steiner

"Angels, Archangels and Archai," "Quiet I bear within me," "Spirit of God" and "Upwards to thee strive the love of my soul." From Steiner 1961. *Verses and Meditations.*

"Hearts that love, suns that warm." From Jones, 1996. *Prayers and Graces.*

"May my heart's warm life," "May my soul's love strive to you," "O Soul in the land of soul" and "To you / In love." From Steiner 1999. *Staying Connected.*

Bibliography

Blake, William. 1988. *The Complete Poetry and Prose of William Blake*. London. Doubleday.

Bittleston, Kalmia. 1983 Oct. *The Threshing Floor*.

Bock, Emil. 1992. *The Rhythm of the Christian Year*. Edinburgh. Floris.

Bock, Friedwart. 2002 Jan/Feb. "Human death and nature's response." *Camphill Correspondence*.

Boogert, Arie. 1986. *Beim Sterben von Kindern. Erfahrungen, Gedanke und Texte zum Rätsel des frühen Todes* [At the death of children, experiences, thoughts and texts about the enigma of early death]. Stuttgart. Urachhaus.

Boye, Karin. 1942. *De sju dödssynderna och andra efterlämnade dikter* [The seven deadly sins and other posthumely published poems]. Stockholm. Albert Bonniers.

Button, Peter. 1971 Nov. *The Christian Community New York Newsletter*. 22.7.

Button, Peter. 1989 Nov/Dec. "Preparing for the End of a Life." *The Threshing Floor*.

Childs, Gilbert and Sylvia. 1998. *The Journey Continues: Finding a New relationship to Death*. London. Sophia.

Crossley, Diana. 2000. *Muddles, Puddles and Sunshine: Your Activity Book to Help When Someone Has Died*. Stroud. Hawthorn. (For children to cope with grief).

Crottet, Robert. 1949. *The enchanted forest and other tales*. London. Richards.

De Hennezel, Marie. 1997. *Intimate death, How the dying teach us to live*. New York. Alfred A. Knopf.

Deverell, Doré. 2000. *Light Beyond the Darkness: The Healing of a Suicide Across the Threshold of Death*. London. Clairview Books.

De Vrieze, Stine. 1976. *De döda kommer en saa nära, Selma Lagerlöfs posthuma novell Själen — verklighetsbakgrund och förhistoria.* [The dead come so near. Selma Lagerlöf's posthume novel *The Soul,* its background and history]. Stockholm. Biblioteksforlaget.

Dominica, Sister Frances. 1997. *Just My Reflection. Helping Parents Doing Things their Way When their Child Dies.* London. Darton, Longman & Todd.

Drake, Stanley. 2002. *Though You Die: Death and Life Beyond Death.* Edinburgh. Floris.

Eckermann and Soret. 1883. *Conversations of Goethe.* Tr. John Oxenford. London. George Bell.

Ellwood, Gracia Fay. 2001. *The Uttermost Deep: The Challenge of Near-Death Experiences.* New York. Lantern Books.

Falkberget, Aasta. 1974. *I Trondalen og på Rotvolden* [In Trondalen and at Rotvolden]. Oslo. Aschehoug.

Gollwitzer, G., Kuhn, K. & Schneider, R. 1958. *Dying we live.* Tr. from German by Reinhard C. Kuhn. London. Fontana.

Hammarskjöld, Dag. 1963. *Vägmärken* [Markings]. Stockholm. Albert Bonniers.

—. 1964. *Markings.* Tr. Leif Sjöberg & W.H. Auden. London. Faber.

Head, Joseph and Cranston, S. C. (eds.) 1985. *Reincarnation. An East-West Anthology.* Illinois. Theosophical Publishing.

Johanson, Irene. 2002. *What The Angels Need to Tell Us Now.* Forest Row. Temple Lodge.

Jones, Michael (ed.) 1996. *Prayers and Graces.* Edinburgh. Floris.

Kearney, Michael. 1996. *Mortally Wounded. Stories of Soulpain, death and healing.* Cork. Marino.

Koster, Margje. 1993. *Why me? Interviews with seven people with AIDS.* Edinburgh. Floris.

Kübler-Ross, Elisabeth. 1973. *On Death and Dying.* London. Routledge.

—. 1997. *The Wheel of life: A Memoir of Living and Dying.* London. Bantam.

Labaree, Leonard W. 1959. *The Papers of Benjamin Franklin.* Vol 1. Yale University Press.

Lennon, John & McCartney, Paul, 1987. *Beatles Complete.* Hal Leonard.

Lewis C.S. 1966. *A Grief Observed.* London. Faber.

Lusseyran, Jacques. 1999. *What One Sees Without Eyes.* New York. Paragon and Edinburgh. Floris.

Madill, Betty. 2001. *One Step at a Time, Mourning a Child.* Edinburgh. Floris.

Moody, Raymond. 1975. *Life after Life.* Illinois. Bantam.

—. 1978. *Reflections on Life after Life*, Illinois. Bantam.

Rittelmeyer, Friedrich. 1937. *Aus meinen Leben* [From my life]. Stuttgart. Urachhaus.

Rozzell, Calvert. 1992. *The Near-Death Experience.* New York. Anthroposophic.

Schauder, Hans & Franke, H.W. 2002. *Vienna: my Home.* Edinburgh. Private publication.

Schilling, Karin von. 1988. *Where Are You? Coming to Terms with the Death of my Child.* New York. Anthroposophic.

Scholl, Inge. 1966. *Den hvite Rose* [The White Rose]. Oslo. Riksmålsforlaget. (The English translation of the book did not contain the part quoted.)

Scott, Gabriel. 1918. *Kilden* [The well]. Oslo. Aschehoug.

Solzhenitsyn, Aleksander. 1971. *Stories and Prose Poems.* London. Bodley Head.

Spect, Richard. 1925. *Gustav Mahler.* Stuttgart/Berlin. Deutsche Verlags-Anstalt.

Steiner. Rudolf. 1948. *Briefe I 1881–1891.* Dornach. Rudolf Steiner Nachlassverwaltung.

—. 1961. *Verses and Meditations.* Tr. George Adams. London. Steiner Press.

—. 1970. *At the Gates of Spiritual Science* (14 lectures Stuttgart Aug 22 – Sep 4, 1906). London. Steiner Press.

—. 1979. *Anweisungen für eine esoterische Schulung* [Guidance in esoteric training]. Dornach. Rudolf Steiner Verlag.

—. 1985. *The Dead are with us.* Tr. D.S. Osmond. London. Steiner Press.

—. 1990. *The Prescence of the Dead on the Spiritual Path.* New York. Anthroposophic.

—. 1994. *The Archangel Michael: His Mission and Ours.* New York. Anthroposophic.

—. 1994. *Theosophy: An Introduction to the Supersensible Knowledge of the World and the Destination of Man.* New York. Anthroposophic Press.

—. 1995. *Life Beyond Death.* London. Steiner Press.

—. 1999. *Staying Connected: How to Continue Your Relationships with Those Who Have Died.* New York. Anthroposophic Press.

—. 2002. *Living With The Dead: Meditations for Maintaining a Connection to Those Who Have Died*. Forest Row. Steiner Press.

Storm, Howard. 2000. *My Descent into Death*. London. Claiview.

Torvik, Kjellaug. 1989 June. Article in *Familien*. Oslo.

Turoff, Stephen. 2000. *Seven Steps to Eternity; The True Story of One Man's Journey into the Afterlife*. London. Clairview.

Uthaug, Geir. (ed.) 1990. *Fyll mitt beger påny* [Fill my cup once more]. Oslo. Lyrikkvenner.

Watson, Lillian Eichler. 1988. *Light from many Lamps*. New York. Simon & Schuster.

Wilder, Thornton. 1947. *The Bridge of San Luis Rey*. London. Longmans, Green.

Wolf-Gumbold, Kaethe. 1969. *William Blake*. Tr. Ernest Rathgeber & Peter Button. London. Steiner Press.

One Step at a Time
Mourning a Child

Betty Madill

This book is an invaluable source of comfort for all those who find themselves grieving for a child. Offering sensitive ideas for dealing with the child's effects or with feelings of guilt and helplessness, *One Step at a Time* combines personal recommendations with practical suggestions for finding bereavement support and counselling.

Betty Madill's advice is touching, credible and sensitive to the individual's need to move on with their life, taking happy memories of their child with them, while working through their debilitating grief.

Betty Madill lost her three-year-old daughter, Lisa, in a swimming pool accident in Brazil in 1983. Her personal tragedy eventually led her to work as a counsellor for The Compassionate Friends, an organization which helps people to work through similar loss.

Floris Books

Though you Die

Stanley Drake

Death is a certainty that affects us all, and that every human being has to face.

More is known about human death than many people realize. A growing number of people have felt themselves to be on the brink of death, and having 'an out-of-body experience.' Some of these people feel they have actually chosen to come 'back to life' after hours on the operating table.

The spiritual insight of Rudolf Steiner shows distinct stages in existence after death. Above all there is the central Christian mystery of death, the full significance of which has not yet been grasped by human thinking and which will only reveal itself as that thinking becomes more spiritual.

Stanley Drake, born in 1906, worked as a priest in Forest Row, Sussex. He died in 1986.

Floris Books